PRO TACTICS™ SERIES

THE FISHING BOAT

Use the Secrets of the Pros to
Select and Outfit Your Boat

David A. Rose

THE LYONS PRESS
Guilford, Connecticut
An imprint of The Globe Pequot Press

This book is dedicated to two very patient women:

my mother, who was willing to drive me to out-of-the-way
fishing holes of my choosing each and every week during
the days of my youth;

and my wife, Carol, who's been putting up with not only
my antics for years on end, but my continued infatuation
with fishing, as well.

To buy books in quantity for corporate use
or incentives, call **(800) 962–0973**
or e-mail **premiums@GlobePequot.com.**

The Lyons Press is an imprint of The Globe Pequot Press.
Pro Tactics is a trademark of Morris Book Publishing, LLC.

Photos by David A. Rose unless otherwise credited

Text design by Peter Holm (Sterling Hill Productions) and Libby Kingsbury

Library of Congress Cataloging-in-Publication Data is available on file.

ISBN 978-1-59921-443-6

Printed in China

10 9 8 7 6 5 4 3 2 1

CONTENTS

ACKNOWLEDGMENTS

You don't write a book alone. Thank you to captains Mike Gnatkowski (gnatscharters.com) and John VanDusen (reelfunfishingcharters.com), both with decades' worth of charter-fishing the Great Lakes; Alton Jones (altonjones. com), Bassmaster Elite tournament pro; and Mark Martin (markmartins.net), the Professional Walleye Trail's (PWT) original champion.

Thanks also to Mark Brumbaugh (markbrumbaugh.com), PWT Champ; Scott Pitser, one of the best flats guides I know (now retired); Ben Wolfe, client and great with a digital camera; as well as David Richey, famed outdoor writer who helped get me into this business.

I also thank Huge Witham (schmidtoutfitters.com), unparalleled river guide; Russ Maddin (231-633-6464), phenomenal river guide; and David Scroppo, one of the best at outdoor writing and who's taught me more about the craft than anybody.

And, last but not least, thank you to Robbie Voss (Lake Ann Marine, 231-275-6226), mechanic whom I'd trust to wrench all my motors; Marty Kovarik, outdoor writer and a wealth of information; Chris Temple (Bert's Custom Tackle, teclausa.com/bert/); and Brett King (Smooth Moves Seat Mounts, smoothmovesseatmounts.com).

The Fishing Boat

For the owners of fishing boats, there are two situations where the word "never" comes into play.

The first: *Never* mock another angler's boat, no matter its size, shape, age, or condition. The fact that these folks are fishing—the very purpose of owning a fishing boat—is what protects them from ridicule. Heck, an old porcelain bathtub powered by nothing more than a dry-rotted wooden

Fishing pro Mike Gofron and his partner motor down Wisconsin's Fox River in a fully rigged aluminum walleye boat.

paddle would have done me well enough in days before I owned a boat. Watching others fish from boats while you're casting from shore tends to make you think this way.

Boats come in all different shapes, sizes, and ages. But unlike an old dog that can't learn new tricks, a well-seasoned boat can be turned into one heck of a fishing machine once properly rigged.

The second: *Never* forget to heed the old adage "Measure twice, cut once" when you have your power drill's bit snug to the hull of your boat, just seconds from pulling the trigger. Whether you're about to buy a new boat or a used boat or have inherited Grandpa's old one, you will want to make sure you've got that accessory in just the right place before you start drilling. No, rigging a fishing boat isn't hard, but it can make even the most laid-back person a little anxious.

Most anglers can't bear the thought of seeing spirals of boat hull peeling off the tip of a drill bit. I, on the other hand, admit that boring that first hole into a new boat is one of my favorite things in life. It means I have just made the purchase of a lifetime—a new boat for the sole purpose of getting out onto the water and fishing with friends and family. And it means I'm rigging it with the modern tools of the fishing trade. How cool is that?

But the process of rigging a fishing boat starts well before boring that first hole. It begins in the early stage of shopping for the boat and accessories that are right for the type of fishing you do. You've got to try out different rigs until you find "the one," then contact the dealer explaining exactly what boat model you want, with how-many-horsepower motor(s), and what type of trailer. This is also the time to have your dealer or professional boat rigger install any accessory you might not want to attempt on your own.

As I age, I realize the installation of some accessories is better left to those with tools that go beyond what my home shop has to offer, or to those who are more flexible physically. Ever see a 300-plus-pound middle-aged contortionist? Watch me with my head squeezed into a boat's storage compartment while attempting to wriggle my arm past my ear, with screwdriver in hand, down through a wad of wiring so as to tighten up a hose clamp of a self-installed bilge pump, and you will see someone attempting to be one. It's difficult to put into words what that looks like to those watching. I've asked my wife to explain to me, but she just can't muster the words. I appreciate that more than you realize, Honey.

Yes, I find some jobs are better left to someone else. But even with that said, I still rig the majority of accessories to my fishing boats myself—with the help of friends, of course. I always have. It's a great excuse to crack open a cold drink with a bud and, through secondary conversation, save the world while pondering over where an accessory should be placed.

■ Great Lakes trolling boats need big motors for long runs to the hole. Here a deep-V gets up on plane while heading out into Lake Michigan off Frankfort, Michigan.

Lesson Learned

Nowadays, my quest for the perfect fishing boat starts like it will for you—perusing the boat shows and marinas, selecting, testing, ordering, and signing on the dotted line. But it hasn't always been that way. I started small, at a young age, and then worked my way up from there. Each boat I have rigged has taught me a lesson for the next one.

The first boat I fished from was my grandfather and grandmother's 12-foot rowboat. Grandpa had it decked out with a pair of oarlocks, oars, and a navy anchor with a too-short length of nylon rope— that's it. I caught my first fish from that boat while sitting on the bench seat in its stern. I was very young, fishing with my father out front of my grandparents' cabin on northern Michigan's Elk Lake.

The boat was still rigged with nothing more than oars and anchor by the time I was old enough that I could set out and fish alone. The boat's small size limited me to row, anchor, and then dabble a worm over the side, or to row-troll a crankbait. Yes, fishing from that tipsy little boat could be frustrating at times, but the lessons learned were invaluable.

The first lesson was to properly attach anchor-to-anchor rope—with a shackle, not a clip or tied directly. I dove to the bottom of Elk Lake more than once to retrieve that old navy anchor after it slipped free of the clip. And every time the wind kicked up, that short anchor rope would stretch out, the anchor would pull free from bottom,

and then I'd be set adrift. Time and time again I'd pull anchor, row back into shallow water, and reset. And as for row-trolling, that grew tiresome on the shoulders and lower back. But I was young and able to row through the pain. Oh, to have had a cushioned seat with a backrest, and a rod holder—that would have been heaven.

By the time I turned teenager, my family was able to afford a small, 4-horsepower outboard. That little motor opened up my world of fishing even more, not only on Elk Lake but in the connecting lakes in the chain, as well.

The second boat I rigged for fishing, again, wasn't even my boat. A friend of mine purchased a 12-foot boat from a friend-of-a-friend for $100. My dad's 4-horse was a perfect match.

As neither my bud nor I could afford a trailer, we, as a team, became proficient at cartopping this boat. With ultimate speed and efficiency, we could toss in fishing gear, outboard motor, and gas tank, and slam shut the hatchback of his Ford Escort wagon. Then we'd flip the boat upside-down, lift it up onto the homemade suction-cupped cartop carrier, and tie it down. Had NASCAR started running races with rowboats tied to the top of their cars, we'd have been top picks for pit crew. Once at a launch, we were just as fast, if not quicker, at launching. I'm still proud of those days.

It was from this boat I discovered that a landing net, with long handle and large hoop, is just as important an accessory as anything attached to the boat with screw or bolt. The discovery came while attempting to land my largest catch ever. I landed that fish, but it was a struggle with the tiny net we had on board.

My buddy's rowboat was the first I'd ever put a drill bit to. We rigged the boat with rod holders—screwing them directly into the aluminum bench seat without reinforcement. Eventually, just from normal wear and tear, the bases of the rod holders pulled free from the seat. I learned to reinforce when accessorizing or pay the consequences later on. After several years of cartopping, I realized just how convenient a boat trailer could be, too.

Then at age seventeen came the purchase of my first boat—a 14-foot rowboat and trailer. The $400 cash deal was a steal.

Over time, that boat took on the look of the pro fishing boats I'd been admiring in fishing magazines. Rod holders; padded high-backed clamp-on seats; a Lowrance Fish-Lo-K-Tor (vintage flasher/sonar), and oarlock transducer bracket; an anchor, with plenty of anchor line and proper shackle—man, I was living the angler's life. I became educated in proper towing—strapping down the boat with tie-downs to keep it on the trailer, and stabilizing my outboard motor to keep it and the boat's transom free from damage. Having a properly rigged boat helped me catch more fish than ever before.

Later, I was able to upgrade. The used pea-green 14½-foot deep-V aluminum with 35-horse outboard and trailer came fully loaded for the era—paper graph, manual downriggers, and more. I was in angler heaven with all these fishing tools at my fingertips. It was my first boat with a steering column, subfloor, and without bench seats stretching from gunwale to gunwale. This meant I could move around the craft freely.

But this boat had its issues. I learned how the steering cables of outboards worked, as the set on this boat eventually needed repair. Then it wasn't long after that before the old outboard sputtered the last rotation of its prop. Unable to find another used outboard compatible with the repaired steering cables, I settled for a tiller-steer model of a different make and horsepower—a 20-horse, I believe.

Now that I was steering from the transom, it was time to remodel the interior. I removed the steering console, which then led to relocating the paper graph and downriggers. When I tore out and replaced a dry-rotted chunk of floor, I was taught the lesson of proper wiring—making sure, when connecting wire to wire, to do it in such a way that it will last for years. The prior owner had connected crucial wiring with an "it-will-do-for-now" attitude, and years of use and towing had caused the connection to come loose. I was lucky to catch the problem while replacing the floor; it would have been a real mess to fix later on.

The boat had its good points, too. The wood floor and oodles of fishing gear made this the heaviest boat I had owned so far, and that made it easier to control in wind and waves.

■ Downriggers, such as these by Fishlander, need to be mounted securely on swivel bases.

I gained more knowledge about trailers and towing with this rig. Did you know that boat trailer wheel bearings need love and attention every once in a while? Two blown bearings taught me this. This was my first roller trailer (versus bunk), and launching was a breeze.

I bought my first new boat when I was twenty-four. The 16-foot super-deep-V aluminum rowboat was as back-to-basics a rig as you could ask for. It was lightweight and a good match with the new roller trailer. This combination allowed me to launch it nearly anywhere.

The boat really scooted along when you hit the gas of the 25-horse tiller motor, even when maxed out with anglers and gear. Although it was not bought with guiding in mind, this is the boat I started that career from. State regulations concerning the taking of passengers for hire, plus inspections by the Michigan Department of Natural Resources, gave me firsthand knowledge of accessorizing and rigging a fishing boat for safety of the driver and passengers. Storing all the equipment, however, was an issue. This boat did not have a single built-in storage compartment. I had to be creative when it came to packing fishing and safety equipment.

My fishing techniques changed as my fishing career progressed, and I found the boat was not right for me anymore. The boat was too light in the bow, and the slightest breeze would grab it and push me off course. This made it difficult to fish from, whether trolling, casting, or still-fishing. The tall, full-length bench seats made it difficult, if not dangerous, for my passengers and me to move around. I was limited to the back of the boat. My clients had to stay put, as well.

I purchased a tiller electric trolling motor, and that helped with boat control, but I was still disadvantaged because I was continuously reaching my hand down to steer the trolling motor instead of having it on my rod and reel where it belonged. With the trolling motor came added weight, storage, and charging of marine batteries. It didn't take long before realizing it was again time to upgrade.

My dream had come true with my next boat—or so I thought. It was a 17-foot deep-V tiller model powered by a four-stroke 50-horse tiller outboard motor. The rig was cradled in a sleek, black, low-slung bunk trailer. The trailer, with frame and tires more heavy-duty than any I had owned before, allowed me to tow my boat greater distances.

There were a lot of firsts with this boat. It was my first with an inboard battery charger, storage compartments, live well, swivel butt seats and captain's chairs, and electric downriggers. Most important, it was the first with a bow-mounted electric trolling motor, and a powerful one at that. It, along with my old tiller electric, gave me newfound boat control. I rigged it well for fishing, agonizing over how and where I rigged each and every accessory. My clients and I caught a lot of fish from this boat.

But I had issues with the main power—it was underpowered for that particular boat. Gas mileage suffered, my time to and from my honey holes suffered, and, had a storm come along while on the water, my clients and I could have been in danger because of not being able to get back to the dock fast enough. I had just learned an expensive lesson—the importance of matching a boat with the right motor the first time around.

My last two boats have been near-perfect for the kind of fishing I do—both 17-foot 10-inch deep-V "walleye" boats with plenty of horsepower in the outboards. The second-to-last was powered with an oil-injected 125-horsepower outboard, and my latest with a 140-horsepower four-stroke outboard. Both boats have been rigged with 9.9-horsepower kicker motors as well as every bell and whistle when it comes to fishing gear, accessories, and safety equipment. I'm towing them with heavy-duty trailers built for the long haul.

It took several weeks to rig each one just right. No, drilling and attaching the accessories wasn't the hard part; taking the time to sit in them and figure out the best location for each accessory was. I am glad I took the time to do things right. I have been, and still am, truly happy with these rigs (unlike some boats in my past).

What's my reasoning for going down boat-memory lane with you? To let you know that when it comes to messing up a perfectly good fishing boat, I have been there and done that. I'd rather you not make those same mistakes I did, but rather rig your boat right the first time around.

It Pays to Rig It Right

If there is anything I've learned from my years of buying and rigging boats, it's just how much I love fishing from them. Don't get me wrong, I enjoy all aspects of fishing—from flinging flies while wading a fast-flowing river, to surf fishing while standing on a sandy beach, to casting hardware from a cement pier. There is, however, something more personal about fishing from a boat. You are sharing a small space with other anglers while attempting to catch fish. As a guide I have found (and my guide friends all agree) that you may start your day not knowing one thing about the people you are to fish with, but by the end of the day they are good friends.

And boat fishing brings all walks of life together. While guiding, I have fished with a fiddle player from Tennessee who's jammed with the Grateful Dead, and with a world-renowned violinist from Germany while on world symphony tour. I've fished with a garbage collector and junkyard owner who for years pinched pennies to save for the trip, and with a retired man who made his millions programming computers in the early '80s. I've fished with a man who worked the dregs in the sewers under the city streets of Chicago, and with a couple of gentlemen on a fishing vacation from the same city who, well, never would divulge their professions. (I know when to

■ Fishing pro Mike Gofron sits while jigging walleye from the bow of his boat.

leave well-enough alone.) We were contained in a small area—casting, trolling, and drifting. None of these people, or I, would have enjoyed the fishing trips had my boat not been comfortable, with gear out from underfoot, and accessories rigged to maximize their efficiency.

At the time of writing this book, I am a ten-plus-year veteran of writing about camping, outdoor cooking, hunting, and fishing; my career has taken me all over the United States and Canada where I have fished from many different styles of boat. I've raced across a reservoir in a bass boat and then fished its waters for smallmouth, largemouth, and spotted bass. I've surfed huge swells of the Great Lakes in a deep-V walleye boat while pulling spinners behind in-line planer boards, and cast crankbaits for the critters in the wild waters of the North. I've drifted silently downstream in a wooden drift boat powered by nothing more than two oars, all the while catching trophy-size brown trout from under downed timber. I've also been jettisoned upstream in a drift boat powered by a jet-propelled outboard, then quietly drifted back downstream while searching for steelhead and salmon. From saltwater flats boats I have cast the shallows of bays and estuaries for an array of fish species, even nosed up to a rocky shoreline of a Kentucky reservoir and fished striped bass. From Great Lakes trolling boats, I have both hung on for dear life while rocking and rolling in building waves as an impending storm grew nearer, and stood

comfortably, as if on dry land, in the stillness of a calm day.

All these boats were rigged to near perfection by their owners, and I have borrowed tips and techniques from each and every one for rigging my last few boats. I want to share these tips and techniques with you so as to keep you from making the same mistakes I did. Your boat needs to be rigged well to help you catch more fish, to stay safe, and have fun. After all, that's what fishing is all about.

Rigging fishing boats is much different than rigging pleasure boats. The owners of large pleasure boats fret over things like matching the color of the coffee maker and curtains to the rest of the interior. Anglers, on the other hand, are concerned with power, boat control, and efficiency while fishing.

Is there such a thing as having too many accessories? Yes—and that's not only my contemplation, but the thought of every fishing professional I have ever asked. Don't fuss over getting every fishing accessory known to man—there is not enough room in any boat for it all. Use the K.I.S.S. Theory (Keep It Simple, Stupid!) when rigging your fishing boat. After all, it is usually the simplest answer to any question that is correct.

And remember: "Hey buddy, nice boat" goes a long way when talking to fellow anglers at the boat launch, and before you send that drill bit spinning, measure twice (three or four times if need be), and bore once.

CHAPTER ONE

Boats: Basics, Selecting, and Purchasing

Searching for that perfect fishing boat, motor, and trailer can be an overwhelming experience, especially for the first-time buyer. There are just so many makes and models to choose from these days. One pass through a consumer boat show or large marina is proof enough. There are boats everywhere, a dozen styles of each kind lined up gunwale to gunwale, glistening under the overhead lights. Sounds like the showroom of a new car dealer, doesn't it? Actually, there are several similarities between purchasing a car and boat—the salespeople, the loan department, the paperwork, it's all the same. So, pick and purchase a fishing boat like you would a vehicle—it's well worth the several-step process.

Step by Step

The first step, the easiest step, is figuring out what kind of water you'll be fishing as well the techniques you'll be employing most. Will it be rivers, inland lakes, Great Lakes, inshore saltwater? Will you be mostly casting, trolling, drifting live bait, fly fishing, or a combination of these?

If you enjoy fishing for trout and salmon while trolling the Great Lakes, then you obviously shouldn't be thinking about buying a boat made for flinging flies while drifting down shallow rivers. The apparent answer would be to buy a boat made for trolling big water. But don't settle with that quite yet; weigh out all of your fishing options. If you also like fishing for walleye and bass from the same waters, then another option might be to purchase a walleye boat, versatile in that it gives you the flexibility to troll downriggers in big water, yet it also works well for casting and live bait presentations.

Yes, there is a lot to think about regarding what style boat is right for you, but once you determine which techniques and waterways you'll be fishing most, the choice will be a no-brainer. Just remember, though, that you'll never find a boat that is 100 percent perfect. I like to go with a lower-percentage rule: If it's about 80 percent what I need, then it's more than likely the one for me.

Next you will need to know your spending limit, and not just for the boat, motor, and trailer, but all the accessories you want to rig onto it. Peruse the marinas, boating stores, catalogs, and Internet and figure out the costs of the accessories you want before you shop for a boat, and include them in the total price.

Inquire ahead of time, too, what insurance will cost for your new, fully rigged boat, and figure that into your budget. You know your financial circumstances better than a boat salesperson, so stick with your plan, not theirs. You don't want that boat to get you into financial trouble later on.

The next step is research—like you are doing right now. Read this book and then read it again, but don't forget to check out periodicals specializing in all the latest boating gadgetry as well as boat design and manufacturing. There are several on the newsstands to choose from, all of which give the details of the latest hull and interior designs, engineering of motors, along with the newest electronic technology. You can also peruse Internet chat rooms specializing in boating and fishing. Fellow anglers are always willing to share their likes and dislikes about their boats. Talk to dealers, and of course, flip through the manufacturers' catalogs to see what each model offers. Call friends and relatives with fishing boats, pitch in gas money and go fishing with them, and/or hire a charter or fishing guide who fishes from a boat similar to the one you are considering. There's no better way to learn what style, hull design, and hull material best suit your needs than hands-on experience.

The Basics of Boat Hulls

One major decision you'll be faced with is what hull shape and material best suit you. Both boil down to a matter of personal preference and practicality. The boats covered in this book are going to have a flat bottom, V-hull, or deep-V hull design, and they will be made of welded or riveted aluminum, fiberglass, or wood.

Hull Shapes

Flat-bottom. Displacing very little water, a boat with a flat-bottomed hull settles mere inches under the surface. These boats excel in "skinny" or shallow water of rivers and saltwater flats. Their wide, flat design makes them very stable in calm water but a rough ride in any kind of waves. High wind, too, can be a challenge, as flat-bottoms are easily pushed sideways. This type of hull, however, gets up on plane quickly, so motors don't have to be as high horsepower as on other boats.

V-hull. This is probably the most common hull design of all modern-day boats. V-hulls displace a lot of water, thus a boat with this hull design sits lower in the water. This can make them more stable. There are so many variations of V-hulls that it's nearly impossible to describe them all. Most bass boats generally have a modified V section, tapering from the bow to a flatter and wider shape toward the stern. The V shape of the bow slices through the water for a smoother ride. A flat area known as a "pad" is built into the stern to add more planing surface, thus

■ Flat-bottomed boats get up on plane fast with lower-horsepower motors and are best suited for skinny-water applications, as they make for a rough ride in waves. Here, guide Hugh Witham runs up the Big Manistee River.

increasing top-end speed. For control, strakes—ridges on the hull running from stem to stern—help control the flow of water under the boat. They also control the movement of air under the hull when the boat is up on plane.

Deep-V. These hulls give the most comfortable ride of the three, especially when running in rough water. Although today's V-hull flattens slightly into a pad area at the stern, the V shape stays relatively sharp throughout most of the hull.

Here too, strakes help control this hull when running at high speeds. This type of hull cuts deeply through the surface water, and spray is pushed out to the side away from the boat. Because there is so much water displacement, it takes a powerful motor to get a deep-V hull up on plane.

Hull Materials

Fiberglass. A boat with a fiberglass hull will be heavy, which consequently makes for a smoother ride in rough seas than in a boat of aluminum or wood. Performance-enhancing curves and depressions can be molded into a fiberglass hull that may be impossible to duplicate in aluminum or wood. Fiberglass, being the least corrosive, is best for saltwater applications. The polished shine of fiberglass might appeal to you if you are into aesthetics.

The multistep process of building a fiberglass boat, as well its weight requiring a higher-horsepower motor to get it up on plane, means a fiberglass boat will cost more to purchase overall. 'Glass is less forgiving than aluminum in that it may chip or scratch if you beach your boat regularly. There are, however, adhesive guards that attach onto a fiberglass boat's keel to protect it from damage. As a safeguard, these guards should be added onto a fiberglass boat, even if you don't think you'll ever be beaching it. Although it can be pricey, cracks and chips on a fiberglass boat can be repaired to like-new condition.

■ Fiberglass boats are heavy and require high-horsepower motors, but they're a more comfortable ride on big water and in big waves. Here, fishing pro Jon Schneider blasts through waves on Lake Michigan's Green Bay.

Aluminum. The most durable of the three hull materials, aluminum can take the abuse of being beached regularly—a quality that anglers in the rugged backcountry of the Midwest and Canada like. If you are into the glitter-filled look of fiberglass but want the durability of aluminum, you're in luck—manufacturers today are painting up some good-looking aluminum boats, with snazzy graphics to match. As of this writing, aluminum boats are less expensive to manufacture than fiberglass boats. In today's economy, however, the cost of metal, including aluminum, is starting to soar and the price of aluminum boats is beginning to rise significantly.

Boats made with heavy-grade aluminum can take the punishment of big water as well as fiberglass boats. Boats made from light-grade aluminum, on the other hand, will weaken after time due to bending and twisting in big waves. Boats made from thinner-gauge aluminum are fine for small inland lakes. When it comes to buying an aluminum-hulled boat, you get what you pay for. You always do.

Wood. There's a charm to wooden boats. They are, for the most part, made by hand by only one or two skilled craftsmen. Some are built elaborately, with strips of inlay along their gunwales and a finish so deep and clear that it looks as though you could poke your finger right into the grain of the wood. Others are rustic, painted by brush, lacking any pretension of fanciness. Wood boat builders can customize width, height, and shape of a boat to best suit the waterway it will be used in.

When it comes to weight, wood falls in between fiberglass and aluminum. As with fiberglass, though, the weight and maneuverability of a wood boat lie within the hands of the designer and craftsman. In the case of wooden drift boats, lighter is better. A meager 150 pounds makes quite a difference when floating down a river only inches deep. Modern-day wood boats, in some cases, are hybrids between wood and fiberglass. Composite hulls are formed of plywood sheathed with fiberglass, or plywood laminated with epoxy, for strength, reduced weight, and improved hydrodynamics.

Whether all wood or metamorphosed with fiberglass or epoxy, the durability and maintenance of wood boats can be an issue. Drift down rivers near my home in northern Michigan, for example—where dense overhangs, barely submerged rocks, and downed trees make passage difficult—and you'll see wear and tear on the boat by the end of the season. Lack of use can be equally destructive: if you don't use a wood boat often enough, the wood dries out and the pores shrink, causing the boat to leak. No matter how much you use them, yearly maintenance is required with wood boats.

Steering Clear

Once you've established hull material, it's time to decide on the layout of the boat's interior and steering setup. Will you want to steer from the transom or nearer the bow?

Not too long ago, boats rigged with up to 50-horsepower outboards were considered the standard tiller-steer models, and anything larger was steered by console, meaning a steering wheel near the front of the boat. Not anymore. Manufacturers have taken note of today's demand for larger and more powerful boats and motors, and the horsepower ratings of tiller-steer models have risen dramatically. An advance in steering and handling of tiller motors is allowing the horsepower ratings of tillers to reach the 200-horsepower mark. Anglers who want the most room possible in a boat can now have plenty of power behind them.

If you prefer navigating via steering wheel, then you basically have the three console types to choose from—single, dual, or walk-through console. Which one's right for you will depend on the style of boat, how much fishing versus family boating you'll be doing, and the environment of the places you'll fish most.

Single console. Of the three, a single console provides the most room to fish and move about the boat, but protects only the driver from the elements. Because of their small size, boats under 18 feet are best suited for single consoles.

Dual console. Dual consoles protect both the driver and passenger from the harsh elements while running. If designed right, the second console will add more storage to a boat with a properly placed glove box, storage compartment in the front, and out-of-the-way storage under it. There are times, however, when a second console can get in the way—when you are in a hurry to get to the back of the boat to net a fish or while casting from the front deck. My suggestion is to go for a dual console only on boats of 18 feet or larger.

Walk-through console. With the hinged center window of its full windshield shut, a walk-through console offers the ultimate in protection from the elements, especially when coupled with side canvas and top. These are nice for die-hard anglers who make long runs, do a lot of trolling in not-so-favorable weather, and who will be doing a lot of boating with the family.

Let the Shopping Begin

Now that you have established the kind of fishing you'll do most, your budget, the hull design and material, and layout, it's time to start shopping around. This is the hardest step, as it takes up a lot of time, and with all the makes and models available it can be frustrating to pick out the boat that's right for you. Just remember to think practicality: There is no one boat to cover all fishing styles and species—period. The more effort you put into shopping around, the better the payoff in the end.

■ Dual consoles protect both driver and passenger from the elements and, if designed right, will add extra storage to the boat. Here, Mike Gofron motors through a river near Houghton/Hancock, Michigan.

The Test Drive

I'm always taken aback when I hear of someone who bought a boat without ever stepping foot into it first. It happens a lot. You would never think of buying a car without test-driving it, or at least sitting in it, would you? My father actually did that with a car he bought back in the mid-'80s. He picked it out solely on color and style. He went to get in and drive it off the lot after signing on the dotted line, and then found he didn't fit into the driver's seat. Like me, he was not a small man. Dad had to call my mother to have her come down to the car dealer to drive the new car home. Yep, Mom was the proud driver of that new car from there on out, and my father got the old one. Whatever you do, do not purchase a boat solely on color and style. Get in, move around, and if possible, take it for a test drive.

Drive It Like You Stole It

I have been complimented by both car and boat salesmen for the way I test-drive. In a car, I'll test-drive as if I were a teenager driving a super-charged sports car with a decal plastered to the back window that says "Get In, Sit Down, Shut Up, and Hang On!" No, I don't drive with reckless abandon, but I do put the vehicle through day-to-day driving coupled with the extreme driving scenarios I could be faced with in the future. I'll punch the gas pedal as if pulling out into heavy traffic, then hit the brakes—hard. I'll turn sharp left, then right, and do the swerve-side-

to-side thing. I will purposely drive down pothole-infested paved roads as well as rutted and washboard-ribbed dirt roads. I do all this to see how the vehicle handles.

During the test drive of a four-door sedan a few years back, with my wife in the front passenger seat and the salesman in the back, I punched the gas while driving over a series of rolling humps on a long straight-away of a deserted road. I hit those heaves hard enough that from the rearview mirror, I could see the salesman's head touch the car's ceiling as his rear end lifted off the seat when the car went into anti-gravity mode. The salesman surprised me with his comment after regaining his composure, "Finally, someone who knows how to test-drive a car." It was one of the nicest compliments I have ever gotten. The car, by the way, handled well, and we bought it. I test-drive a boat the same way. You should, too.

Insist on taking any boat you are considering for purchase out for a spin, to find out how the boat handles, if it will fish well, and if it's coupled with the right motor and trailer.

The first thing I do is take note of how easy the boat launches off the trailer. Will the dealer need to adjust the bunks or rollers, or will an entire trailer upgrade be necessary? As you'll read later, the right trailer can make or break your day.

Next I start the motor, back away from the dock and out of the way of the launch, and then place the motor back in neutral. While afloat, with the motor warming up, I go through the motions of every conceivable fishing scenario I can think up. I do this untied from the dock, as docklines affixed between the dock and boat will tighten and keep the boat from rocking as it would in the open water.

I move to the bow and make casting gestures (or better yet, I actually have a rod with me). Is there plenty of room to move about? Is there anything like bait wells or consoles that get in my way? Then I stoop down to see how easy it is to get into all the storage compartments.

I'll then make my way into the back of the boat and do the same. Does the boat feel tipsy when I move around? I put the salesperson to work and have them move around the boat while I'm sitting still. Does it rock much when they're walking, stepping over, or leaning? Next, I take a look to see if all my accessories and fishing equipment will fit on, in, and around the boat. It's surprising how different a boat, and the amount of room in that boat, looks while on the water versus in the showroom.

Now I hop into the captain's chair and mess with all the buttons, toggle switches, and controls. Are they easily accessible? Of all controls, the throttle, trim and tilt switches, and horn should be within easy reach. These are all details that would have been overlooked had I not gotten into the boat.

Now it's time to drive, and the more people in the boat, the better the test. The weight of others helps me know how the boat will react with the weight of gear, accessories, and fellow anglers, and

if there is enough power in the motor to handle it all. It won't be the perfect weight distribution (marine gear—anchors, batteries, electric and kicker motors, fishing equipment, and a full tank of gas—will be weighted differently throughout the boat once it's loaded), but it will give me a better understanding of how the boat will react with more weight.

I drive that boat like I would test-drive a vehicle. With everybody seated and hanging on (and with life jackets on), I punch the throttle and see how easily the boat comes up onto plane. If it lacks the power to plane quickly, then I know I'll need to increase the horsepower of the main outboard. I steer the boat from side to side while at high, medium, and slow speeds to see how well the hull digs in while turning.

Then I slow the motor down to an idle. How slow does the boat go with the motor at idle? This is important information if you plan on trolling. If it doesn't troll down to less than one mile per hour, then the boat's a candidate for a kicker motor (low-horsepower outboard) or accessory to slow the boat down.

If the weather allows, I do all the aforementioned high-speed and slow-trolling maneuvers in both calm and rough seas, as the boat will react differently under each circumstance.

One of my most memorable boat test drives was while checking out a 17½-foot aluminum boat on a protected bay of Lake Michigan. When I first saw this boat on the dealer's showroom floor, I thought this could be my next boat. Thank goodness I took her out for a test drive.

It was a cold, wet, and windy day when two salesmen and I launched. I put the boat through the aforementioned test-drive riggers. We were soaking wet by the time we came back to the dock, not just from the rain, but from the spray coming over the bow from the waves. The boat was roomy and the motor was plenty powerful enough, but the hull design made for an uncomfortable, dangerous ride in semi-rough seas. Needless to say, that test drive was the crucial point in my decision not to buy that boat. I would have been very disappointed with the outcome had I not. As you can see, test-driving is crucial.

Now I know it's not always possible to get a boat onto the water for a test drive. If that's your case, then at least get into the boat at the dealer or boat show. Get in and go through the motions of fishing. In fact, get your fishing buddies or the whole family in there with you (yes, even the kids),

■ When test-driving, make sure all controls and toggle switches are within easy reach of the driver.

and all of you go through the motions. Cast pretend rods and scoop fake fish with an invisible net. Move around—a lot. You will at least know how much elbow-room that boat has, whether the compartments and controls are easy to access, and whether the seats are too high, too low, or just right. And you'll know what you do and don't like about the interior of the boat. Remember, no boat is perfect. Even though my present boat is my favorite so far, there are features in it that I am not 100 percent pleased with. But because I got in the boat beforehand, they were not a surprise later on.

Accessorizing Overview

The cliché "a boat is nothing more than a hole in the water into which to throw money" is only a truism if you are not careful about how you shop for boat accessories. This doesn't mean you need only buy the bare essentials, but you do need to purchase the right gear the first time around rather than being frustrated with them later on. I've been dissatisfied with accessories so many times, as were my friends, family, and guiding colleagues. It has ended up costing us more money to replace the substandard equipment than it would have been to rig the boat up with the right stuff the first time around.

Boats, motors, and trailers are going to be with you for many years. As for accessories, they can be upgraded as technology advances. Research, test-drive, and then choose wisely. And by all means, take your time. You want to be the angler who says, "I love my boat, I truly do!"

CHAPTER TWO

The Bass Boat

Bass boats are the ultimate in ultra-fast floating platforms for fishing. When at full throttle with a high-horsepower outboard, these boats fly—literally—over the water's surface at speeds so high it can be hard to breathe. As far as their popularity among anglers, bass boats rank near the top. Why? Bass, especially largemouth, are one of the most sought-after gamefish in the United States, and the above-mentioned speed is appealing to the new generation of anglers.

But there's more to these boats than just a fast ride across a body of water. Their hull design also allows you to access out-of-the-way places—to fish areas so secluded and quiet that your lure's splash on the surface is all you hear. From small ponds to expanses as large as the Great Lakes, chances are you'll see someone fishing from a bass boat at any given time.

Fiberglass is the favored hull material for bass boats, with a design between a flats boat and deep-V. The design lets you fish the shallow water of a backwater bayou, yet allows for a comfortable ride while surfing swells over deep water.

A bass boat's hull is designed to produce lift while the boat's up on plane, similar in theory to airplane wings. Lift allows the bow to rise up off the water, reducing drag to only the rear quarter, thus increasing speed. When coupled with a 250-horsepower outboard, for example, even the heaviest 21-foot fiberglass model can reach speeds nearing 100 mph. Speeds of this caliber, however, are desired more by professional tournament anglers rather than the weekend warrior.

Why the need for such speed? Tournament anglers may travel 100-plus miles one way to get to a spot discovered while pre-fishing, and that doesn't leave much time for fishing during an eight-hour event before having to turn around and make the long trip back to the weigh in.

But such high speed is not necessary for some anglers, and a smaller boat with lower horsepower might be a better choice. A 19-foot bass boat with a 150-horsepower outboard can reach comfortable running speed in the mid-50-mph range and is less expensive than the larger pro models. Whatever caliber

■ Low gunwales are just part of what helps make bass boats the ultimate fishing platforms. Here, Bassmaster Elite Pro Alton Jones attempts to land a jumping smallmouth from Michigan's Elk Lake.

the bass boat, it should be coupled with the maximum horsepower, or close to the highest horsepower the boat is rated for.

There are aluminum models being produced, but the flat-bottomed jonboat-like hull design of these boats limits them to small waterways. On the positive side, a lightweight aluminum boat can be powered by a smaller outboard than heavier fiberglass models, making for an economical ride overall.

Navigation while under power of the main motor will be by steering wheel from either a single or dual console. In a bass boat, dual consoles are desired and take up the least amount of room as compared with all the other boats I'll be talking about in this book; their cockpit-like area for driver and passenger sits low, well below the front and rear fishing platforms.

Jack plates are common on most bass boats. You can tweak out speed and performance by lifting and lowering the outboard with these. Jack plates will be explained in detail in chapter 7.

Because of their excessive speed, bass boats are one of the few types of fishing boats I suggest accessorizing with foot-pedal throttles and foot- or steering-wheel trim and tilt controls and jack plate controls, rather than the standard throttle lever with trim/tilt toggle switches. It's much safer to keep both hands on the steering wheel at such high speeds.

All Hands On, and Below, Deck

Every bass boat owner I've ever known says the two most important features of their boats are the fishing platforms and the storage within them.

Both bow and stern platforms, or decks, are really what make fishing from a bass boat what it is. The openness, with low gunwales and cockpit-type consoles, means anglers can move about the boat easily and cast and retrieve lures in a 360-degree circumference without anything in the way. When shopping for a bass boat, make sure there is plenty of length and width in the bow area to be comfortable while moving about. The majority of time spent in a bass boat will be on this front deck and, at times, by more than one angler.

All that deck area makes the size and placement of storage compartments, live wells, and coolers within bass boats some of the best designed. But even with that said, when shopping around, you'll want to make sure the manufacturer has utilized the space well. Storage is a necessity, not an option. Due to high speed and low gunwales, rods, tackle, and personal gear can easily be blown out. You'll want to make sure all gear is stowed or strapped down when running. Storage compartments are so roomy in some pro models of 20 feet and larger that tournament anglers are able to carry a spare bow-mount trolling motor and the tools to change them out. Yes, this may be out of the league of most anglers, but you get the point of their storage capacity. Gear stowed out from underfoot will make you a more efficient angler, as well.

Bass Boat Accessories

Bass boats are among the easiest to rig, as they require few accessories; most of the fishing will be hands-on techniques like casting, drifting, and, when fishing for panfish, rigging or drifting live bait.

A bow-mounted electric trolling motor is a must. But don't let the motor's name fool you—you'll be doing little trolling from this type of boat. A bow-mounted trolling motor, however, is the primary source of control over a bass boat's position while fishing. Trolling motors should be as high-pound-thrust you can afford—a 24-volt to 36-volt system with at least 100 pounds of thrust.

A large drift sock is standard equipment for boat control, as well. This will slow down your drift during the windiest of days.

Bass boats should be rigged with sonar and GPS units in two areas—either two separate units or an all-in-one—on the console and on the bow. An in-dash sonar and small GPS unit mounted on top are a good choice for small bass

boats, as space on their consoles tends to be limited. The console sonar's transducer should be mounted either amidships with through-hull puck-style, or externally on the transom. A powerful sonar, and GPS if desired, should be mounted on the bow where it can be seen easily by the angler operating the electric trolling motor. The bow sonar should be attached to or built into the bottom of the trolling motor.

Keep a set of marker buoys on hand in the bow, too, even if there's a GPS up

▥ A retractable strap for holding equipment, such as these muskie rods and reels, is a common accessory on bass boats. Unstrapped, these rods could fly out of the boat during a high-speed run.

there. It's tougher to stay over structure while watching a GPS than it is a well-placed buoy.

Have a Seat

For the most part, what you see for the driver and passenger seats are what you get, as these are built into the flooring. Just make sure they have plenty of padding and are high backed.

The bow pedestal seat and hydraulic post should be of high quality, and if not, should be upgraded. Most fishing will be done from a standing position in bass boats, so "pro" or butt seats are desired. One at the bow is pretty standard protocol. Similar seating on the rear platform for your fishing partner adds a nice touch.

Your fishing rods also need a place to sit. The placement and quantity of rod holders on a bass boat, though, will be at the discretion of the boat owner. In my neck of the woods, for example, where dragging tubes in deep water for smallmouth bass is a common ploy, two rod holders on the gunwale near the bow and two at the stern are an asset. On the bass boats of those who also fish crappie in the reservoirs of the South, you'll see several rod holders on the rear gunwale and on the transom. If you employ only hands-on techniques, you may find you want no rod holders at all.

Other rod holders you'll like are for holding rods down while running, rather than having to tuck them into a rod storage compartment. Hook-and-loop-type straps, built-in retractable straps, and bungee-cord style are all fine. Rod straps lessen the time spent storing equipment before running hole to hole.

Bass anglers of yesteryear very rarely anchored when fishing; a navy-style anchor with at least 100 feet of anchor line was kept on board only as safety equipment. That, however, is starting to change. Alton Jones, Bassmaster Elite pro from Waco, Texas, brought power poles (automatic anchor poles) to my attention. "My power pole's become a more important tool on my bass boat than my trolling motor," he told me. These devices, which deploy from the transom with just a button's push, will hold a boat in position in shallow water in even the strongest wind and current. They are becoming standard equipment on bass boats of the South.

CHAPTER THREE

The Drift Boat

The fish that inhabit rivers have no idea how beautiful a home they have. I, on the other hand, as an angler who targets them while floating down rivers in a drift boat, sure do. Drift boats are among the most unique fishing craft made—they are designed to take you to waters inaccessible by any other type of boat or even by foot.

The environment of a river is ever-changing—banks erode, overhanging trees uproot and tumble into the flowing water, boulders inch their way downstream, and sand and silt are continuously on the move. Within days, what was once a deep hole can fill in and turn into a shallow run. Even anglers who fish a river often never really know what to expect around the next corner. The shallow draft of a drift boat makes it the ideal craft to maneuver in such varying conditions. Drift boats can be as simple as 10- to 16-foot craft powered by nothing more than a pair of oars, to larger boats motorized by the most powerful inboard, outboard, and jet-drive motors money can buy. Whether built by a large manufacturer or in a small shop by a lone boatbuilder, the best type of drift boat for you will vary according to the region where you live and fish, and the size and flow of the particular rivers you'll be fishing. From shallow rivers so narrow you could easily cast across them, to rivers so deep and wide they resemble flowing lakes, there's a drift boat built for each one.

No matter the style, however, drift boats are designed to do one thing—to float within only the top few inches of water so as to allow the current to flow under you without grabbing the boat and pushing you downstream.

The question of what hull material is best for a drift boat to be constructed of—wood, aluminum, or fiberglass—has been a great debate among anglers for years. Drift boats have been built out of wood since the first one was conceived, and wood drift boats are still sought after to this day. They are a classic by design.

In contrast, the shape a fiberglass hull can be molded into is limited only by the imagination of the builder, thus making it a good choice for drift boats that will be pushed about by high-horsepower motors.

Drift boats with aluminum hulls have the least amount of maintenance and are economical to buy.

■ Guide Hugh Witham nets a Big Manistee River steelhead for Russ Maddin.

How you rig your ideal drift boat depends on the river and type of fishing you will be doing most.

Small Drifters

In the late 1800s, in the cold-flowing waters of Michigan, the Au Sable river boat—a narrow, 20-plus-foot drift boat, with a shape resembling a canoe—was commonplace for anglers who fished the river of the same name and the nearby Manistee River. Because of their sleek shape, these boats maneuvered well through the riverbank's thick overgrowth. Today, the traditional wood Au Sable river boat is still being produced, but appeals mainly to those looking for the nostalgia of days gone by while fishing these famed rivers. The river environments, along with anglers' methods, have changed since those early days, and so too has the design of the drift boats that float down these waters.

Drift boats, in general, are now wider to enhance stability, allowing you to stand while fishing, and are shorter for improved maneuverability around tight corners. Wood, aluminum, and fiberglass versions of McKenzie River (Western-style) and Midwestern-style drift boats and dories, along with hybrid versions of these and others, are seen floating down rivers today.

Being light in weight is crucial with small drift boats, as sections of river may be only inches deep. Rowing, too, is easier in a lightweight boat—the oarsman may have to suddenly stop the drift of the boat with only one or two strokes of the oars before ramming into a newly formed logjam.

Inside Accessories

Storage compartments within small drift boats are few, as the extra weight of the material used to build them is unwanted. Whether built into the boat under a seat or a dry box on the floor, one dry-storage area for life jackets and extra clothing is all that's desired.

I strongly suggest folding seats, padded and with back, for both anglers and rower. Just make sure the seat on the rower's bench swivels and has enough elbow-room to allow full strokes of the oars. The boat should have sturdy stanchions—devices for leaning into while standing in the boat—in the bow and stern.

Center Stage

The rower's area in the center of the boat is where most accessories will be found. Their actions need to be immediate to avoid obstacles, keep anglers within casting distance, and maneuver the boat when fish are hooked. Everything needs to be at the fingertips of the rower.

Anchors, anchor-rope systems, and oars are the most-used items in a drift boat.

The anchors used on drift boats differ from those used on other boats. Most drift boat anchors are heavy, 30 pounds or more, to give them a solid hold on the river's bottom, yet designed without flukes to keep from getting caught on debris when it's time to move. They grab hold as sand and gravel wash out from under them, settling into the bottom and silt. Solid lead pyramid-shaped anchors are popular, as well as several short lengths of weighty chain, or a combination of the two.

One of the most important accessories is an anchor system that allows a quick lift and drop. Pulley systems in which the anchor rope weaves through to a bracket and roller on the bow are the most common. The anchor line—supple and at least ½-inch-diameter woven nylon—is held in place by a quick-grip cleat that's within arm's reach of the rower, or by a crimping-type stopper, also called a jam or cam cleat, if a toe-release is used. Today's market has an array of manual anchoring systems available to choose from. Which is better for you is a matter of personal preference.

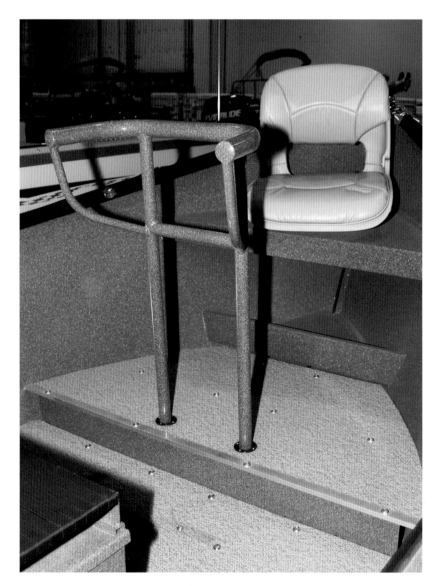

■ A stanchion, such as this one, is an important accessory in a drift boat, keeping anglers comfortable and safe.

■ A river is ever-changing, so the rower's actions need to be immediate to avoid obstacles. Here, guide Russ Maddin rows his drift boat, avoiding a collision with a downed tree.

Stroke, Stroke, Stroke!

Well-made oars are not an option with drift boats—they are a necessity. Their size (length) will depend on the size of the drift boat. Oars can be purchased in wood or composite materials. Composite oars, however, are desired as they are both strong and lightweight. Heavy-duty oarlocks, well beyond what's found on a rowboat, are equally as important. Emergency break-down oars are available and a good investment. Accidents happen—a broken oar or one lost and floating downriver out of reach is a possibility.

The oars themselves should be accessorized. Oar stops (large rubber O-rings to keep oars from sliding out of the lock) and devices to keep them in an upright position while in the oarlocks, Oar-Rights, make life much easier for the rower. On the oar handle, foam hand grips will prevent blisters; and on the blade end, tip protectors are suggested, especially when fishing shallow, narrow rivers where oars are continually hitting obstacles.

Small-Boat Comfort

Nothing makes for more uncomfortable fishing than wet feet—a good possibility in small drift boats. An inexpensive manual bilge pump will siphon water out quickly. Rubber interconnecting floor mats, too, are a nice option, as they'll keep your feet and fishing equipment up off a wet floor. Rubber, however, is heavy

and may add significant weight to a small drift boat.

Other accessories to include are: fish box, if catch-and-keep is your thing, to fill with ice and keep kept fish fresh; and cup holders to keep things neat and tidy.

Rod holders, too, along the rear gunwale and across the transom, are needed if you are going to be pulling plugs (crankbaits) or drifting live bait. Make sure they are removable, though, as fly anglers will get frustrated if fly lines get tangled in them (as they have a way of doing).

Large Drifters

The bigger the water, the larger the drift boat—a larger boat means more power both in propulsion and accessories. As with any boat, the main motor should be as close to the maximum horsepower the boat is rated for, especially if you choose jet over propeller propulsion. If you intend to troll, and the boat's transom is large enough, a kicker motor is an option, as well.

My suggestion for steering a large drift boat would be a powerful motor via steering console nearer the bow, rather than from a tiller motor at the transom. Rivers are narrow bodies of water, and it's much easier and safer to be able to see what is ahead of the boat without another person's head in the line of sight.

■ Pyramid-shaped lead weights and chains are anchors unique to drift boats.

■ A quick-grip cleat within arm's reach of the rower keeps a firm hold on a drift boat's anchor line.

Big Drifter Accessories

The aforementioned accessories of small drift boats can be used on larger drift boats, too. But the larger boat, powered by motor with marine batteries on board, increases the amount of accessories you can add.

Instead of manual lift anchor systems, the addition of a marine battery allows for power lifts. Multiple toggle switches can be wired into the boat, including one on the steering console, one on the floor by the rower's feet, and one up in the bow.

Downriggers can be rigged onto drift boats—placed on the gunwale at the rear or on the transom, along with extra rod holders in the same area.

Sonar and GPS units should be placed on the steering console within easy view of the driver. Secondary all-in-one units can be added on the transom for those who troll with downriggers.

A bow-mounted trolling motor is a welcome addition if there's going to be any casting done in slow-flowing rivers or

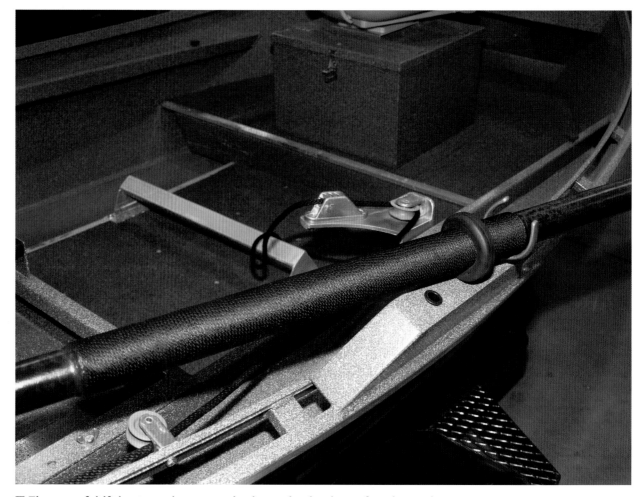

▦ The oars of drift boats can be accessorized to make the chore of rowing easier.

their backwaters. Just remember that electric motors and especially the marine batteries add a lot of weight.

If you plan on fishing rivers during cold-weather months, then you'll want to consider a drift boat with a cabin area. These are popular on waters where steelhead and salmon run in the fall, winter, and spring months when air temperatures may drop to below freezing.

CHAPTER FOUR

The Great Lakes Trolling Boat

Ever wanted to put your place in this world into perspective? Troll the Great Lakes to the point where land is just a small line on the horizon, if not gone altogether, and you will.

Trolling big water calls for a big boat. No, you don't need a 50-foot yacht to enjoy a day on the Great Lakes, but for safety's sake, you don't want to be out in the middle of one of these massive bodies of water in

■ Two fully rigged Great Lakes trolling boats head out to fish off the Lake Michigan port of Michigan City, Indiana.

a rowboat. Whether made of fiberglass or aluminum, a wide-beamed deep-V hull is the way to go. I've trolled for brown trout from a 17-foot aluminum deep-V in a bay of Lake Michigan in water so calm you had no reservations about being there. I've also trolled salmon in a 25-foot fiberglass boat while 12-plus-foot Lake Michigan waves crashed over its enclosed bow. That was one wild ride; one that made me glad to be in a boat of that size. There's no rule for what size boat you should be in while fishing the Great Lakes, other than to respect the water

by being in the proper size boat and proper hull form for the conditions at hand.

When trolling, you and your fishing partners will be spending most of your time in the stern; a boat with room enough to hold several anglers in this area is a must. The boat's gunwales and transom need to be wide to accommodate equipment.

Motors for the Long Run

Great Lakes trolling boats are one of the few fishing craft where the type of main

■ Great Lakes trolling boats should have a wide, open stern area, as this is where all the action takes place. Here the author (left) has just fought and landed a Lake Michigan lake trout off Michigan City, Indiana.

motor—inboard, inboard/outboard (I/O), or outboard—is a major decision. It's a matter of having enough space both in the stern and off the transom.

Inboard motors—with the motor under the floor—allow the maximum amount of floor space as well as room for trolling accessories off the transom. Most charter captains prefer inboards for this reason, since they need extra room not just for gear but for fighting and netting fish in a stern crowded with people.

With inboard/outboards, however, the housing cover over the motor takes up some room in the stern, and you'll have to work around this. I/Os are best suited for trolling boats of 20 feet and larger.

An outboard motor, in contrast, allows full use of the stern area, but takes up valuable space at the transom that could be used for trolling accessories. Outboard motors are better suited for small trolling boats where room for anglers to roam is at a premium.

Make sure to max out that boat's horsepower rating, as long runs to and from fishing spots are common on the Great Lakes. It takes a lot of power to get a deep-V boat up on plane, and as you'll read later, the savings in fuel will be noticeable, as well.

Accessories for the Trolling Angler

A kicker motor is suggested anytime you head out onto a large body of water. If your main motor fails, battery power runs out, or you run short on gas, that little pull-start motor will get you back to shore. Kicker motors, too, will troll down to a creep, whereas the main motor may not.

Bow-mounted electric trolling motors are a great option for small, open-bow trolling boats. They can be used for a stealthy troll in shallow water where fish can spook easily. In early spring on the Great Lakes, for example, brown trout cruise in water as shallow as 4 feet deep. Even the smoothest-running gas motor will alert these fish of your presence, and they'll quickly head for deep water. The near-silent hum of an electric trolling motor is perfect for pulling lures in this situation.

Electric trolling motors can pull a boat at speeds slower than a creep, making them perfect for trolling Great Lakes' walleye with spinners (crawler harnesses). They also allow a small-boat angler to hover over schools of fish, like perch and whitefish, for still-fishing and vertical jigging techniques, and for casting lures in shallow water.

Sport fish can be found in most any section of the water column within the Great Lakes, so it's the goal of most every trolling angler to get as many lines out as possible—high, low, and everywhere in-between—without tangling. There are plenty of devices you can use to get lines spread out away from the boat and down into the depths.

Outriggers are long fiberglass poles that extend outboard from the gunwales,

■ **A fully rigged trolling boat includes kicker motor and steering rod.**
CHRIS TEMPLE

holding trolled lines out away from the boat. A closed loop of line, extending from the base to its tip, is woven through a pulley on the outer end of the outrigger. In the same manner as raising a flag on a flagpole, multiple fishing lines, held to the looped line by releases, are spread out for trolling alongside the boat. A pair of outriggers, one on each side, attached to the gunwales about amidships, is typical rigging.

Planer boards—devices that plane off to the side of a moving boat—are standard equipment on Great Lakes trolling boats.

They come in an array of shapes and sizes, from small in-line models that attach directly to the trolled fishing line, to large wooden or composite contraptions that are tethered to the boat by 150-pound-test thin-diameter woven-nylon line. With these full-sized boards, the trolled fishing line is attached to releases that are free-sliding on the nylon tether. These boards can be a chore to pull in and out of the boat without a planer board mast. Reels on the mast allow you to quickly wind in the large planer boards. Masts, for the most part, are bolted into the floor in the bow.

Downriggers—essential tools for precision depth control—are the most common accessory on Great Lakes trolling boats. How many and whether electric or manual models depends on how deep your pockets are. Their position on the boat, however, is a matter of room in the boat. On a large trolling boat with an I/O motor, multiple downriggers can be placed along the transom. Four 'riggers are commonly seen here on many charter boats. On small trolling boats with outboards, two downriggers, one on each side on the rear gunwale, is customary. These downriggers on the gunwale are common on large trolling boats in addition to the transom units. All downriggers on gunwales need to be mounted on swivels.

Hold It!

Of all accessories, rod holders are the most important on Great Lakes trolling boats. The biggest problem of most new-boat owners is they don't realize just how many rod holders they really need. A properly rigged trolling boat will have dozens of fully adjustable rod holders rigged throughout the boat, most concentrated from amidships to stern. Open-bow trolling boats necessitate a few up front, as well.

Why so many? Trolling anglers need empty rod holders ready to go—just as many without rods in them as with rods in them—for when fish are hooked. Things get crazy when a fish is on and rods need

to be cleared out of the way, but not pulled completely. Rods with line still being trolled can be moved over to the empty rod holders so as not to get tangled up. After the fish is in the boat, you just move the rods back to their original spots.

Rod holders should be heavy-duty and fully adjustable. The torque placed on rods while in downriggers or while using diving apparatuses (like Dipsy Divers) is great, and wimpy rod holders will break. And there are so many different techniques used while trolling that holders need to be able to swivel side to side and forward and back in unlimited number of positions.

Track systems that work in conjunction with rod holders are becoming more popular than ever. Tracks reduce the need to drill the many holes needed for individual rod holders.

"Rocket launchers"—rod holders that keep unused rods upright, tangle-free, and within easy reach, placed in out-of-the-way areas—are found on many trolling boats. On large boats, these apparatuses are usually attached to the back edge of the top over the console or up front in open-bow boats.

Rinse, Repeat

Great Lakes trout and salmon can be awfully slimy critters, and goo and mire go everywhere as these fish wriggle in the net in the bottom of the boat. A raw-water wash-down—basically a bilge that pumps lake water through a hose and nozzle—is great for immediately cleaning up the mess for those who like to keep things tidy.

■ Rod holders on Great Lakes trolling boats should be all the same brand and model as well as fully adjustable, as there are many different techniques used at one time.

A clean floor will also save you from a slip and a fall.

Electronics for the Troll

Knowing your exact location, the depth of the water you're fishing, the speed at which you're trolling, as well as the water temperature at the surface and the temperature break (thermocline) at all times are the quintessential elements for a successful day on the water. This makes quality electronics—sonar, GPS, and speed and temperature probes—the essential tools for trolling success.

Depth and Navigation

Sonar and GPS are important fishing and navigation tools of the Great Lakes trolling anglers. Most agree that two separate sonar and GPS units—an all-in-one unit and a GPS unit, for example—on the helm is a better choice than just one unit. It's easier to see two separate, larger screens than one smaller screen divided in two. As for safety, if one unit breaks down, you at least have a GPS to get you safely back to port.

Secondary sonar mounted on the transom is a nice touch for anglers working the downriggers, as they can see depth changes and fish firsthand, and they can quickly make adjustments.

Temperature and Speed

Water temperature is the telltale factor as to where Great Lakes fish will be located in the water column, making a temperature/speed gauge a must for anglers who troll here. There are several different kinds on today's market, including probes that hook in-line to downrigger cables and transmit temperature and speed to a monitor on the dash. The speed sensors of these probes give the most accurate indication of how fast your lure is being pulled through the water, as water current down deep changes with the wind. Your boat may be trolling at 2 MPH on the surface, but due to water current down low, your spoon's not working right because it moving at 3.5 MPH.

Handheld models that read water temperatures every 5 feet are available, as well. These can be clipped onto your fishing line, lowered by the downrigger, and then retrieved and read. Handhelds, however, are limited to temperature only.

CHAPTER FIVE

The Saltwater Flats Boat

I'm always amazed at what skinny (shallow) water a saltwater flats boat can navigate in. "If designed right, they can float on spit," says retired fishing flats guide Scott Pitser. Because of their shallow draft, saltwater flats boats are able to take anglers to water other types of boats can't reach. When rigged correctly, they are the ultimate boat for making a stealthy approach at fish feeding in the shallows.

There have been plenty of changes in the design of saltwater flats boats over the past decade—they're lighter in weight, more stable than ever, and their hull design's been tweaked for improved performance. Although you may see an aluminum hull floating around your favorite estuary, fiberglass is still the most sought-after hull material due to salt water's corrosive properties.

To keep things simple, I'll be relating to two popular flats boat designs—the skiff, which has been in style for decades, and the newly admired bay boat.

Skiffs are flat-bottomed boats built to skim the surface water when running, and then settle mere inches into the water while being fished. Their width and wide gunwales make them very stable boats.

But skiffs aren't popular only with saltwater flats anglers. That flat-bottomed bow works well for anglers who nose up to shore and anchor, as well. Many striped bass guides who fish steep-banked reservoirs with live bait techniques, for example, use skiffs as the boat's flat shape at the bow snuggles up nicely to the shoreline; they're as stable as a well-built dock. Nose up to shore in a V-hull, and the boat will rock side to side with every move made.

The flat hull design, however, makes for an uncomfortable ride in rough water—a dilemma for flats anglers who have to make long offshore runs to and from fishing grounds. Bay boats, on the other hand—with their modified V-hull design in the bow that tapers wider and flat at the rear—are coming to the forefront as a rough-ride remedy. But this modified hull design doesn't allow bay boats as shallow a draft as skiffs.

One key feature to look for in a flats boat is plenty of waterproof storage compartments, as the hands-on techniques anglers use from flats boats call for gear to be put away and out from underfoot. Wide gunwales provide storage room for rod tubes under them, helping to keep things untangled and safe from breakage.

Instead of bilge pumps, most flats boats have a self-bailing system. It's imperative that these are designed well to keep water off the floor.

Accessorizing

The primary means of fishing from flats boats is sight-fishing—spotting fish, and then maneuvering the boat to within casting distance of fish so as to make a cast.

Most of a flats boat's accessories are geared toward this.

Because of surface glare, the best vantage point from which to spot fish is as high off the water as possible. A platform—the most noticeable feature of saltwater flats boats—is constructed in the rear of the boat and allows the spotter/pole person a 360-degree view of the surrounding area. Platforms should be large enough to allow spotters to shuffle their feet around without fear of falling, with a raised lip around the edge so as to warn, by foot, that the edge is

■ Flats boats are open, no-frills boats perfect for casting and fighting fish.

▥ Flats boats aren't just for salt water. Here, a striper guide bellies his skiff up to shore, its flat-bottomed hull design perfect for the job.

there. Platforms should also have adequate drainage grooves keeping them free of standing water. There should be plenty of steps to mount and dismount safely.

Another option for spotting fish is a tower constructed over the center console; the spotter simply climbs to the top and peers out into near-shore water. As of this writing, however, the jury is out on whether towers are here to stay or just a fad. Towers add significant weight to the boat, and the theory of "If you can see the fish, they can see you" comes into play.

Once fish are spotted, then maneuvering the boat to within casting distance without spooking them is the name of the game. Bow-mounted and tiller-steer electric trolling motors and push-poles are essential for stealthy boat control.

The flat-bottomed design of flats boats makes them vulnerable to being blown around in strong winds; thus it is easier to pull or push a flats boat with a powerful trolling motor in these conditions. Hand-controlled trolling motors are desired, as the salt water is guaranteed to play havoc with foot pedals. Remote-controlled trolling motors—operated with a handheld device about the size of a car's remote key fob—are efficient for spotters on a platform or tower. Due to fighting incoming and outgoing tides throughout the day, electric motors need to be at least 24- to 36-volt systems for power and battery life. Even though today's electric motors run quieter than ever, many flats anglers feel the push-pole is still the ultimate tool to silently maneuver through shallow water. Most guides use both electric trolling motors and push-poles throughout the day.

For the angler in the bow, a pro or "butt" seat on an adjustable pedestal is recommended. There are times when you've just got to lean back and take a load off.

Electronics

Seeing as much of the fishing is done in such shallow water, sonar units need not be extravagant when fishing saltwater flats. One unit at the dash—in-dash being a popular choice due to limited space on the console—is sufficient. In flats boats used in waters other than saltwater flats, such as the aforementioned striper fishing, sonar is more important for marking bait and fish under the boat, and a powerful unit is desired.

GPS, on the other hand, is an important tool for getting to and from fishing areas safely. One unit mounted onto the top of the steering console within easy sight of the driver is common.

Anchors Aweigh!

Anchoring is a common ploy for flats anglers. Even though most fishing is done from shallow water, a heavy anchor with plenty of anchor line is needed. A fluke-style anchor with at least 100 feet of rope (for safety) will work fine. Some flats anglers, however, prefer the Cajun-style anchor—a 4-foot steel rod with an eyelet on one end to attach the anchor line, which is thrown into the soft bottom like a spear. Power poles—an electric pole anchoring system that extends straight down off the boat from the transom—are becoming all the rage with saltwater anglers, as they can be deployed with just a push of a button from nearly anywhere in the boat.

Nice Performance

As flats boats get larger and heavier comes the need for performance-enhancing accessories for both boat and high-horsepower motors.

Jack plates not only improve overall performance when running, but allow the motor's lower unit to be lifted up and off bottom in shallow water. Lifting the motor reduces the chance of damage to the prop and lower unit and saves native shallow-growing grasses from being torn up. Tilting the motor lifts the lower unit, but it does so at such an angle that it pushes the back of the boat down farther into the water—a hindrance in shallow water.

Trim tabs are popular among saltwater flats boat anglers, as they help lift the

■ Poling platforms should have a raised lip running all the way around, as well as plenty of steps to the top. Here, guide Chris Jones poles through a saltwater flat near Islamorada, Florida.
BEN WOLFE

stern when getting up on plane, and keep it up when running in shallow water. With a quick adjustment via a console control, trim tabs will also smooth out and level a flat-bottomed boat's ride in rough water.

Keep It Clean

A raw-water wash-down—basically a hose and nozzle—to clean fish goo from the deck is a nice feature, especially for flats anglers who catch their own live bait (nothing makes a bigger mess faster than a cast net full of wriggling shad). An immediate wash-down of fish slime not only makes the daily chore of cleaning a saltwater boat easier, but keeps anglers safe from a hard slip and fall on the boat's fiberglass floor.

Rod Holders

How many rod holders a flats boat should have, and their placement, depends on the type of fishing done from a flats boat. Most fishing techniques are hands-on-rod methods, so when sight-fishing saltwater flats, few, if any, rod holders are required. For flats boats used on waters other than saltwater flats, rod holders may be an important accessory. The striper anglers mentioned above use up to a dozen rods at a time, so many on the rear gunwales and transom that their boats resemble a porcupine with its quills erect.

"Rocket launcher"–style rod holders, on the other hand, which hold rods upright and out of the way while fishing, are common on flats boats. These holders are usually found on the front of the console or on the platform.

CHAPTER SIX

The Walleye Boat

The walleye boat, in my opinion, has been incorrectly named. Sure, it's the perfect boat for fishing walleye, but it really should be called a "multi-species" boat rather than just a one-species vessel. Versatility is the very reason I have chosen this style of boat for personal use.

■ A fiberglass walleye boat in the morning mist. Here, walleye tournament angler Scott Rhodes (bow) bottom-bounces for walleye in Michigan's South Lake Leelanau with his dog, Hogan, and Dave Scroppo.

As with most other boats, aluminum and fiberglass deep-V walleye boats are being built larger, both in width and length, than ever before. These big boats are allowing anglers to explore farther out into big water, as well.

Power Kick

Although inboard/outboard motors can be found on some Great Lakes models, outboards are by far the more popular means of powering a walleye boat. As these boats increase in size and weight, so too does the horsepower of the outboards needed to push them. Tiller versus console steering is a matter of how much room an angler wants in the boat.

As I have said about every boat in this book so far, the motor needs to be as close to the maximum horsepower rated for the boat. On the transom of professional tournament anglers' 20-plus-foot boats you'll find 225- to 300-horsepower outboards, the higher pushing a 21-foot deep-V upwards of 60 MPH. My current

■ A fully rigged walleye boat from the rear shows its kicker motor and powerful tiller electric trolling motor.

17-plus-foot deep-V with 140-horsepower outboard (only 10 horsepower under the maximum rated for the boat, mind you) top-ends at 42 MPH. For inland lake anglers, 16- to 17-foot models powered with 60- to 90-horsepower motors are a popular choice, topping out at speeds in the low to mid-30s.

Walleye boats coupled with outboards of 80 horsepower and higher should also be rigged with a 6- to 9-horsepower kicker motor, as these high-horsepower main motors won't be able to troll down slow. An extension handle on the kicker allows an angler to stand or sit trolling. These make it easier, too, to control your kicker while holding your boat in position over deep water when vertical jigging. If steering via the console is more your thing, then linkage rods for simultaneous steering of the main motor and kicker are a good choice.

Inside Job

Walleye boats probably come in more styles than any other boat—from "pro" models with wide gunwales to attach accessories, and plenty of storage compartments and bells and whistles, to smaller "guide" or "outfitter" models with thinner gunwales, similar to heavy-duty rowboats, with less storage and fewer frills. Then there are single, dual, and walk-through consoles to choose from, again a personal choice between roominess and protection from the elements.

Accessories for the Walleye Boat

Wow, where to start? With so many techniques used to fish walleye, let alone the multitude of other species that can be fished from this style of boat, walleye boats are heavily accessorized.

The most used accessory when fishing walleye is rod holders. A walleye boat should be loaded with them, along the gunwale from bow to stern, plus a few at the transom. My boat, for example, has twelve bases in which I can attach my eight rod holders. The four up at the bow work well when bottom-bouncing, deadsticking, or trolling with lead core or divers, while those nearer the stern can be used for the aforementioned as well as when trolling crankbaits or in conjunction with my downriggers. There are two on the transom for trolling giant lures in the prop-wash for muskies (muskelunges).

Hello Down There

Walleye anglers use their sonar often, for spotting fish, bait, and structure, thus a powerful large-screen unit is preferred. Two sonar units—one at the bow and one on the console or within easy sight of the driver of a tiller-steer model—is the norm.

GPS, too, is used heavily by walleye anglers, not only to get to and from fishing hole and launch, but to troll an accurate path along a breakline or previous path where fish were caught. Whether two separate units or an all-in-one unit is up to the angler.

■ The self-adjusting steering rod sits between the main motor and kicker motor.

Control for More Fish

Electric trolling motors, both powerful tiller models and bow-mounted models, are used often by walleye anglers. The bow-mount is used for nearly every application—from slow-trolling spinners, to bottom-bouncing, to casting—and tillers for back-trolling with a live bait rig, a very popular ploy of walleye anglers. Depending on the size of the boat and the amount of room for marine batteries, both trolling motors should have 24- to 36-volt systems.

Downriggers, too, are a common accessory on walleye boats. If you only fish walleye occasionally with them, then manual 'riggers will suit you well. If you'll be fishing with them often, including doing much trout or salmon trolling, then you will want to consider electric 'riggers.

Little Things Mean a Lot

Drift socks, marker buoys, and the like are used often by walleye anglers, and both should be within easy reach, not tucked away in the bottom of a storage compartment.

Splash guards—rubber or Plexiglas flaps that attach to the transom—are an accessory geared specifically for walleye boats. These keep an angler dry when back-trolling in rough water, and keep large waves from washing over the transom when trolling or when quickly decelerating after a fast run. A sudden wash of water over the transom can stall out motors and short out batteries.

Most walleye boats come with high-back padded seats, including the one for the bow area. In the case of trolling, bottom-bouncing, and live bait rigging, it's nice to be able to sit down and fish. On the other hand, if you want to do any casting from the bow, then a "pro" or butt seat on a hydraulic pedestal is suggested.

A bimini top is a nice accessory when fishing in the rain or under a hot sun, especially if you are going to be fishing with kids. Biminis can get in the way in certain circumstances, as when casting lures or when trying to net fish.

■ Walleye boats should have a powerful bow-mounted electric trolling motor. Here, David Anderson fishes walleye on South Dakota's Lake Francis Case below the Big Bend Dam.

CHAPTER SEVEN

Main Power

If there is anything I want you to get out of this entire book, anything at all, it is this: Do not underpower your boat with too small a main motor. All fishing boats need to be powered by a motor as close to or, better yet, the maximum horsepower the boat is rated for—period.

A powerful motor will get your boat up on plane quickly and give it maximum speed when loaded with anglers and gear. You'll also have a noticeable savings on gas consumption.

Don't Be Fooled

Beware of "low-monthly-payment" boat, motor, and trailer deals; dealers tend to package these with low-horsepower motors, well under the maximum the boat is rated for. I've made this mistake. What could have been the perfect fishing rig was turned into a very expensive lesson in underpowering a fishing boat.

It was the purchase of a 17-foot deep-V tiller boat and 50-horsepower four-stroke outboard motor—the boat, mind you, was rated to take up to a 75-horsepower motor. The boat was a sharp-looking,

seaworthy vessel, and I rigged it with every bell and whistle an angler could want. As for the motor, it was one smooth-running machine at both high and idle speeds. I loved it.

Four-stroke outboards were the new engines on the block at the time; the allure of this particular combo was that it should be much better on gas consumption than my previous two-cycle outboards—about 20 percent better, to be exact. But reduced gas consumption was never achieved.

Individually, both boat and motor were as good as one could ask for. Unfortunately, they were not a good match with each other. The boat was underpowered with this size motor. It would get up on plane when I was by myself, but not quickly. With another angler on board, it was a guessing game of not just how long, but whether the boat would get up on plane at all. Conditions had to be perfect. To achieve plane I'd have to aim the boat with the wind and hit each wave just right, all the while my fishing partner and me shuffling our butts around in the seats to get our body weight distributed correctly. With three anglers aboard, or two anglers and a live well full of water, forget it—getting the boat on plane was only an aspiration. With the added weight, the boat's hull would plow though the surface, not on it.

As for top speed, I could get her up to 29 MPH with just myself in the boat—not bad for a heavy boat and a 50-horsepower motor. With two other anglers, on the other hand, its speed would plummet. According to a client and his handheld GPS during a guide trip, our speed was an embarrassing 11 MPH. Gas mileage

suffered terribly with more than one person in the boat.

The one thing most people do not realize is that the money spent up front by going for the maximum power a boat is rated for will, in the long run, come back double in the money saved on fuel. And with gas prices soaring ever higher these days, the savings may be even more.

So how does a higher-horsepower motor equal better gas mileage? The motor does not have to work as hard to get the boat up on plane; once on plane (and

■ All boats should be powered with the highest horsepower motor the boat is rated for. Here, a deep-V, fully loaded with passengers and gear, is easily pushed through high waves on Michigan's Lake Gogebic.

this is where the real gas savings occur), you are able to let up on the throttle, lower the RPMs by a couple thousand, all while the boat stays on plane. You'll cut your gas consumption by nearly half by letting up on the throttle after the boat's up on plane.

Motor Types

The main power for a fishing boat is going to be an outboard, inboard, or stern or inboard/outboard (I/O) motor.

Outboards

Without exception, the outboard—engine and propulsion in one self-contained unit—is the most popular overall; these motors are easy to work on and require less maintenance, especially when storing them during the off-season.

A lot has changed with the outboard motor since the first two-cycle model was invented in 1909. Gone are the days of simple carburetors and air intakes. Instead, when you pop the cover of a new outboard, you'll find fuel-injected systems and computer-chip technology. Not a bad thing, unless you are a fix-it-yourself kind of person. The ease with which an outboard motor starts up on a below-freezing day, on the other hand, makes me glad for every wire, port, and microchip in my outboard motor.

There are two main types of outboard motors you have to choose from today—four-stroke and oil-injected. Which type of outboard is right for you is a matter of

personal preference as well as regulations of the lakes you'll be fishing. Some waterways, for instance, have four-stroke-only regulations. If there is any chance you will be fishing one of these regulated lakes, then the answer to which type of outboard for you is obvious.

Four-strokes. These are popular with anglers looking for a quiet, fuel-efficient ride that has little impact on the environment. My boat, for example, is powered by a 140-horsepower four-stroke and even when at full throttle, two anglers can talk and be heard without as much as a holler. As a guide, I find this silence adds to the tranquility of fishing the clear waters of northern Michigan, and the motor's low emissions help keep the waters pristine.

Instead of instant acceleration when the throttle's punched, a four-stroke has a smooth increase in speed. Some four-stroke manufacturers, however, have added superchargers to their four-strokes, giving them a neck-snapping acceleration when the throttle is goosed. Unfortunately, gas mileage suffers when the supercharger kicks in.

Four-strokes, overall, tend to be heavier than other outboards, a consideration if you are looking to put one on a lightweight boat. Engineers, however, are designing more powerful and lighter-weight four-strokes than ever before, and the models coming out in the near future will be impressive, I'm sure.

Oil-injected. The efficiency of gas consumption and emissions of today's oil-injected outboards is improving by leaps and bounds, as well. While not nearly as loud as they once were, oil-injected outboards do have a slight rumble to them as compared to four-strokes. I like an outboard with a little roar to it on the back of a bass boat. Perhaps it's the similarity between the "on your mark, get set, go" of bass tournaments and stock car racing, or maybe it's just what I am accustomed to; either way, I dig it. Oil-injected outboards have instantaneous get-up-and-go, making them a good choice for heavy boats.

One downside of oil-injected outboards is the oil itself—you have to add oil to the reservoir on a regular basis, and there is that added cost.

Inboards and I/Os

Inboards and inboard/outboards (I/Os) are common among big-water anglers who troll, as they allow maximum use of the transom for fishing equipment.

Inboards. With engine and drive gearing under the boat's floor, inboards are most commonly found on large 20-plus-foot

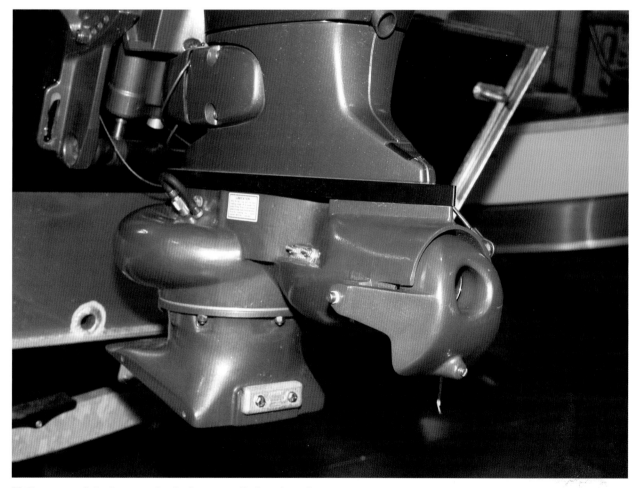

■ Close-up of the lower unit of a jet-propelled outboard motor.

vessels. Many charter captains prefer inboards, as they allow the most room for passengers to move about aft. The low center of gravity created because the engine is within the hull makes for a stable ride.

Inboard/outboards. I/Os are a combination of inboards and outboards—with the engine in the interior of the boat and an outboard drive unit through the boat's transom—and are again popular with anglers who fish big water but from mid-sized boats. As with inboards, an I/O's engine is low and centered in the boat, giving the craft greater stability. Some walking room is lost in the stern area due to the engine's cover protruding through the floor.

Forward Ho!

The next thing to consider is the type of propulsion—propeller or jet—that best suits your fishing. Just in the sheer numbers of what's on the water, propeller propulsion by far outnumbers jet propulsion. But popularity alone does not necessarily mean prop propulsion is a better choice. It is all a matter of the waters you will be fishing most.

Jet Propulsion

Basically, jet motors propel a boat by sucking in water through a large-diameter inlet in front of the lower unit, via a large spinning impeller in a water pump, and then spitting it out through a smaller-diameter nozzle in the back. Only a jet motor's intake needs to be underwater, making jet-propelled motors sought after by anglers who need speed in extremely shallow water. This specialized shallow-water application is most popular with river anglers. Jets are trendy with the environmentally minded as well, as they do not tear up vegetation like a propeller does.

In the days of two-cycle outboards, jet outboards were known as obnoxiously loud motors due to their exhaust port being out of the water. The quietness of four-stroke outboards, however, has made that a thing of the past.

Jet-powered motors should be of the highest horsepower you can afford, as jet propulsion is less efficient, power-wise, than prop propulsion. Another downside of jet drive is you'll have to be careful not to let the lower unit touch the river or lake bottom, since debris, such as gravel, twigs, and fishing line, can be easily sucked into the unit, jamming the impeller and quickly putting the motor out of commission.

Propeller Propulsion

Knowing an entire book could be written on these spinning, multi-bladed devices, I'll cover propeller propulsion in a generalized manner. The basics are this: The horsepower created by the engine is transferred to a spinning propeller to create thrust. There are several options in the material, diameter, cup, rake, and pitch that will change the speed, load capacity, and handling ability of a boat.

Propellers are made of three materials, aluminum being the most common.

Aluminum propellers offer reasonable durability for the average angler and can be easily repaired if damaged. Stainless steel is the strongest material, which may increase speed and efficiency due to the stiffness of the blades, but can be costly to repair if damaged. Composite propellers, made of a tough, lightweight material, work well as an emergency prop, but can be considered a throwaway if badly damaged.

The diameter of a propeller is the measurement of the width of its circular shape from blade tip to blade tip as the propeller rotates. A propeller's diameter will be a fairly standard measurement for the particular motor you are using.

Pitch defines the angle of a propeller's blade that, in theory, equals the distance a propeller would move a boat with one full rotation. Slippage, however, comes into play when pushing a boat, thus some forward motion is lost. The lower the pitch, the less forward motion a boat will have in one rotation of the propeller. Lower-pitch propellers, on the other hand, have more power for getting your boat up on plane quickly or for when pulling water-skiers. A 19-pitch prop, for example, would theoretically move forward 19 inches with one rotation; a 21-pitch prop would theoretically move a boat 21 inches with one rotation. You'll see an increase of about 1½ MPH with the higher-pitched prop. An increase in speed, though, depends on many different factors of the design of the prop and boat hull design. Your boat's shot-out-of-the-hole speed, on the other hand, will

suffer with higher-pitch propellers. Pitch is the first thing to consider when a boat is not performing as you would like it to.

The *rake* of a propeller is the measurement of the slant or inclination of the blade from the gearcase.

The *cup* is the curved lip added to the tip of a propeller's blade. A cup can increase rake and pitch of a blade.

Most boat manufacturers have determined what combination of propeller characteristics is best for each boat model when matched to an engine of the maximum rated horsepower. Your boat and motor dealer should be able to help you with those statistics. But never assume that the propeller that is on a motor, even if on a package deal, is the perfect one for the boat you are purchasing. Insist on taking and changing out propellers while test-driving. Try out propellers made from different materials and with diverse pitch. You'll be surprised at the outcome. Purchase the propeller that best performs with the boat.

I suggest the purchase of a second propeller, extra pins, and hub assembly—in case you severely damage or lose the original propeller—at the time of the original acquisition of the motor. And carry the spares in your boat, not in the vehicle, so that you can replace them on the water, allowing your safe return home.

Motor Accessories

There are many accessories for motors on the market today; some allow you to slow a boat down to a troll, some improve high-end performance, and others protect the motor itself from damage.

Foiled Again

Hydrofoils are fishtail-looking devices that bolt onto the motor's gear-case cavitation plate in a horizontal position, adding lift to the stern and eliminating bow rise while the motor is under high power. This allows your boat to get up on plane faster and curbs hopping or "porpoising" as well as cavitation. Some models require additional stabilizers, as there is noticeable torque to the steering when a hydrofoil is rigged, especially with tiller motors.

Trolling Plates

Are you fishing from a mid-sized boat with a motor that won't idle down to trolling speed? If so, a trolling plate may be in order. A trolling plate is basically a flat piece of composite material that drops into a vertical position behind the propeller to block thrust. This is completely different from a jack plate, which lifts the motor straight

■ A trolling plate in the down position. Trolling plates allow a boat with a larger motor to go slowly enough to troll.

up and down on the boat's transom. The trolling plate allows the boat a slow troll with the motor running at a higher RPM. This increase in RPM reduces spark plug fouling, as well.

Trolling plates come in two basic styles—manual and spring-loaded models. Manual units are raised for running and lowered for trolling by the angler via a lever and stainless wire. Spring-loaded models, on the other hand, lift (push out) automatically via the thrust of water when the prop is rotating at high speed. The device then drops into the down position at low speeds.

The spring-loaded version is suggested for the forgetful—those of you who may not remember to lift the plate before running. Forgetting to lift the plate may not only damage the device itself, but over time, may also damage the motor's shear pins. One downside of all spring-loaded trolling plates is the loss of thrust while in reverse. This will make docking difficult.

Guardian Angels

Running in shallow water means damage to a motor's propeller and/or skeg is a possibility. Damage to either will put a quick end to a fishing trip and be costly when repaired. Skeg and prop guards rigged to a lower unit will help protect a motor from such damage.

Prop guards do just as their name implies—guard the propeller from damage due to hitting an obstruction. There are several styles of prop guards on the market, ranging from rings which act as a shroud around the entire propeller, to flat horizontal fins fitted over the skeg which have a plate that lies flat under the propeller.

Prop guards take the punishment of hitting an object, and the force of the hit lifts the lower unit up, thus the propeller rides over the obstruction rather than rotating through it.

Skeg guards protect the *skeg*—the lower unit's rudder hanging below the prop—from wear and tear and accidental breakage. Whether made of stainless steel or composite materials, skeg guards wrap around the skeg and increase its overall strength.

Accessorizing for Performance

Trim and tilt, and, depending on the boat, foot throttles, jack plates, and trim tabs are all essential tools for gaining better performance from your motor.

Trim is the positioning of a boat, horizontally, in the water. *Tilt* moves the motor by angling it forward and back, which lifts the lower unit up and down at a slant. The correct trim when powering up on plane—lower unit forward so as to keep the bow down—and then the slight adjustment of trim once up on plane, is of the utmost importance in the speed, efficiency, and handling of your boat. The amount of gear, passengers, and fuel—and their placement—will vary each time out on the water, so a boat's trim will vary every time out, as well. Tilt is used when motoring in shallow water or to position the motor when towing.

Hydraulic trim and tilt is pretty much standard equipment on most large motors. My suggestion, though, is to accessorize with trim and tilt on any size boat and main motor—even a motor as low as 15 horsepower. Trimming and tilting a motor will increase performance and handling of even the smallest boats. Trim and tilt, however, needs to be hooked up to a battery, and so should be used on motors with electric start.

The trim-and-tilt toggle switch should be easily accessible by the driver. Most are located on the throttle lever. On high-speed boats, such as bass boats, a trim-and-tilt switch attached at the steering wheel is suggested. Another suggestion for fast boats is a foot-pedal throttle rather than the standard throttle lever. Keeping both hands on the steering wheel at all times is much safer than one hand on the wheel and one on the throttle and trim-and-tilt switch, especially when running in rough water.

Tweaking Performance

Jack plates should be considered for high-horsepower outboards. With these you will obtain peak speed, out-of-the-hole performance, and better gas mileage. A jack plates lifts an outboard motor straight up rather than tilting its angle, allowing the boat's trim to stay the same, great if you'll be running in extremely shallow water

and need maximum clearance between the lower unit and bottom. Jack plates come in manual or power lifts. Power jack plates—controlled by a switch at the steering column—are most common, as they can move a motor into different positions while running.

Trim Tabs

Another device, or pair of devices, is trim tabs. Mounted under the waterline on the back of the transom, trim tabs can be individually adjusted up and down to level out a boat while running, or help you get up on plane faster. At one time, trim tabs were found only on large big-water vessels. However, over the past few years they have been modified to work on smaller fishing boats. Trim tabs are controlled by a small panel of buttons that should be mounted within easy reach of the driver. Models that automatically rise when the motor is turned off are nice, as they will save you from tearing them off the boat should you forget to raise them before putting the boat on the trailer.

Gauges and Meters

Instrument gauges and meters for your boat motors are just as important as they are on the dashboard of your towing vehicle. They give readings of how your motor's running, oil pressure, temperature, and the like, as well as indicating positions of trim and tilt and jack plate. Some are complex, literally computers in themselves that communicate with the computers in your motor, deciphering everything from the basics of fuel consumption, to hours used, to informing you when it's time to change lube and oil, to actually allowing you the ability to change the RPMS your motor is running. The very basic gauge clusters you should consider include gas gauge, speedometer, tachometer, battery voltage, and oil pressure.

Ever fish at night? If so, you know how difficult it can be to see beyond the lights of a brightly lit dash. One thing I highly recommend on fishing boats is that the gauges be backlit by red or blue lighting rather than the standard bright white lighting, since colored back-light won't ruin your night vision. Another option is to install a switch to turn off the gauge lighting while still being able to run bow and stern lights. In the past, I have used a thick dark-colored towel with hook-and-loop tabs on the corner that I stick to corresponding tabs on the dash to cover my gauges at night—a simple, quick fix until the dash can be properly wired.

Tips for the Long Run

The ultimate goal of any angler is to have a main motor that never gives any trouble—to start when needed and to run smoothly

■ Jack plates can help tweak the performance of outboard motors.

for years to come. The simple process of following the manufacturer's scheduled maintenance program is the most important thing any angler can do to lengthen the life of their outboard. Yet these simple tasks are often overlooked.

The oil and oil filters in four-stroke motors should be changed in accordance to the manufacturer's guidelines, as well as the oil in all motor lower units. Spark plugs should be inspected monthly and replaced every year. The belts of inboards need to be periodically inspected and replaced as needed.

The impellers of water pumps for cooling systems are the most overlooked of any part of the motor. These need to be replaced every two years. These days it's a $20 part plus labor to replace the impeller—or $200 in parts and three times the labor, not to mention likely damage to the motor, if you wait until it fails and you have to make repairs.

A water separator attached in-line with the fuel line should be rigged on every boat and motor that's used in environments where temperatures change dramatically throughout the day. In my home state of Michigan, for example, morning air temperatures might start out at 30 degrees and then rise to 75 degrees later in the day. This much fluctuation in temperature is guaranteed to produce condensation in a fuel tank. Water in gas-station pumps is a common cause of poor-running motors, as well. A water separator is one of the all-around best accessories you can add to ensure a smooth-running motor. Make sure to change the filters in water separators often.

Additives for cleaning fuel systems of boat motors should be used periodically. If your motor's not going to be run for a month, then a gasoline stabilizer—not only added to the gas tank, but run through the motor—is in order. Today's gasoline is not the same as your father's gasoline; it's more volatile than ever and breaks down fast. One-month-old gas is now considered old.

CHAPTER EIGHT

Accessorizing for Boat Control

Obsessed with finding that one magic lure or bait? Forget it. Boat control is really the most important aspect of catching fish.

I've seen it time and time again—clients pulling their boat north for a week's fishing, on vacation with their buds, who have hired me at the beginning of their trip to show them all my honey holes. I don't hold anything back. I show them every weed bed and log- or rock-strewn area. We fish. We catch fish. My clients mark their maps and punch coordinates into their GPS units.

But I am the one in control of the boat during the guide trip, be it by electric trolling motor, gas kicker motor, drift sock, or combination of the three. My clients are fishing and memorizing how they should get back to the spot while I maneuver around structure. But I'm adamant about teaching them everything they need to know about catching the fish from the waters we're fishing. I talk about how to use their accessories for boat control, including what to do in case of a change in weather.

I conclude the trip with a chat about the day's fishing—on the wheres, whats, and hows of the day so my clients can enjoy a fish-filled trip throughout the rest of the week. I insist they call me and give me a report on the fishing and catching. If they don't, I'll call them.

When we finally connect, the conversation usually goes something like this: "We went back to all the spots you showed us several times during the week, cast the same lures, even tried a few of our own techniques, but we just never hooked up with anything." I know what their problem was. It almost always boils down to improper boat control on their part. They may have had a bow-mounted electric trolling motor but never used it; they may have had a drift sock but never deployed it; they may have had a kicker motor, but instead made too fast a trolling pass with the main motor. Needless to say, their catch ratio suffered. You see, boat control is essential to catching fish.

Accessories for boat control should be priority one. Powerful electric trolling motors, gas kicker motors, drift socks, oars, and push-poles are all important equipment.

Electric Trolling Motors

If a fishing boat has room for marine batteries, then by all means it should be rigged with an electric trolling motor. Electric trolling motors offer anglers superior boat control and can get you into areas inaccessible via the main motor. They run nearly silently, allowing you to sneak up on fish without them ever knowing you are there.

Voltage and Thrust

The number-one rule when purchasing an electric trolling motor? Always purchase one with the highest pounds of thrust and the largest voltage system that your boat can support.

How high a voltage you should have will depend on the size of your boat and how many batteries it can store. A 12-volt trolling motor runs on one 12-volt marine battery, a 24-volt system requires two separate batteries, and 36-volt system needs three. Small boats, let's say 14 feet and under, can get by with a 12-volt system, while 16- to 18-footers should have at least a 24-volt motor. Anything larger will require a 36-volt system. Most manufacturers have designed their boat's battery compartments to hold the proper amount of trolling motor batteries needed to best power the boat. But never assume they

have. Make sure your boat can handle the motor and batteries before you purchase them.

Thrust is the amount of propulsion of an electric motor. The higher the volt system, the more pounds of thrust a motor has. High-thrust trolling motors have the power to buck a headwind or hold steady in river or tide current without having to be at full power. Having leftover thrust will allow you an extra boost of power when you need it—and I guarantee you, at some point in time throughout a day's fishing, you will need it. Today's trolling motors are more powerful than ever, yet have been engineered to produce more pounds of thrust while using less battery power. This is very noticeable in comparison to electric trolling motors of just a decade ago.

The longevity of battery power is another reason to purchase as high a voltage system and as much thrust as you can. A high-thrust trolling motor doesn't have to work as hard as one with too little thrust, thus less power is drawn from the batteries. Also, the more batteries you have connected to the motor, the longer they'll last. With 24- and 36-volt motors, only a small amount of power is drawn from each battery rather than all the power being drawn from one single battery. The higher the voltage of a trolling motor, the more batteries, and the longer it can run before draining the batteries dry. I have found, in general, that I get a day's worth of juice from a 12-volt system, two days from 24-volt, and three days from a 36-volt system. This, of course, depends on how hard the motor worked when used in high wind or in heavy current.

Choosing the Right Motor for You

A well-built trolling motor is a must, as these devices take a lot of abuse. Ramming into boulders and stumps and scraping rocky bottoms is nothing unusual during a day's fishing. Look for units with a composite or stainless-steel shaft. Make sure the unit has a weedless propeller, one for which replacements can be easily found in stores. If you'll be fishing salt water, make sure you purchase a trolling motor made specifically for this application, with internal electronics sealed to protect them from corrosion and outer components that won't oxidize.

Bow-Mounted Motors

Bow-mounted trolling motors provide the utmost in boat control, as they pull rather than push a boat. This is especially noticeable in windy conditions.

But before going out and purchasing a powerful bow-mounted trolling motor, make sure your boat was built to handle it. Most of today's boats are manufactured with a flat surface on the bow that has been reinforced to handle the torque of high-powered trolling motors. On some boats, however, you may have to reinforce the bow area with another layer of plywood or composite material. I once had a manufacturer custom-make another bow platform

that I screwed right onto the existing one because the original platform would bend under the torque of the motor at full thrust. When I goosed the juice, the motor would literally lift the platform, and the base of the trolling motor would tilt to the point that the shaft would cock to nearly 45 degrees. I lost forward motion and boat control, to say the least.

Quality electric trolling motors will come with the proper hardware and instruction for proper placement. Follow the instructions to a T, and you should have no problems.

One trolling motor accessory I have found useful is a quick-release or sliding bracket that attaches between the motor and platform. Quick-release brackets are nice for taking the motor off for servicing, towing, or when your boat is parked in an area where thievery is a problem. Sliding brackets, which also act as a quick-release, allow you to slide the motor forward while in use, then slide it back for docking, towing, and covering with the mooring cover. Nice.

Size Matters

A trolling motor's shaft length is the next thing to consider. Too short a shaft, and your trolling motor's prop will pop out of the water between waves, and you'll momentarily lose boat control as well as forward momentum.

A prop should be at least 1 foot below the bottom of the boat when lowered all the way down. On boats with high bows,

■ A bow-mounted electric trolling motor rigged onto a sliding plate, in the storage position.

■ Proper shaft length of bow-mounted electric trolling motors is crucial for proper boat control. Here, even the longest shaft made pops out of the water in high waves while fishing pro Mark Brumbaugh fishes Michigan's Lake Gogebic.

such as deep-V hulls, this requires a motor with a shaft of at least 60 inches.

On the other hand, put a trolling motor with too long a shaft on the bow of a boat with a low-profile hull, such as a bass boat or a saltwater flats boat, and the head of the trolling motor will be too high on the platform and get in the way when casting. Before you bolt that new trolling motor to your boat's bow, make sure it has the right size shaft for your vessel.

Keep Control

Bow-mounted trolling motors can be controlled in a variety of ways, including foot-pedal-, hand-, and remote-control steering.

Foot-pedal Steering is desired by anglers who do a lot of casting, as they are able to keep their hands on their rod and reel at all times rather than reaching for a control. With foot-pedal models, you'll have the choice of electronic versus cable steering. Cable has an immediate response to steering—you push the foot pad forward or back, and the cable linked between the control and motor directs the motor right or left. The high-profile forward/back toggle of a cable-steer pedal, though, does take some getting used to. Some boat manufacturers have built a recessed area into the bow platform to accommodate the height of these foot pedals.

The low-profile left/right toggle pedal of electric steering, however, is nice for those who have a hard time with the pedals' height and forward/back pivot, and works well for boats that do not have a

pedal alcove in the floor. With modern electric steering, the delayed response of the signal from the foot pad to the steering of the motor is barely noticeable.

The long cord of electric steering allows you the freedom to control the boat from most anywhere in the boat. All that cord, however, will take up room on the boat's floor. Remote-control foot pedals are making their way to the fishing scene to remedy the wad of wiring. Just make sure to stow these wireless foot pedals in a compartment before making a high-speed run, as they can easily be thrown from the boat. Few saltwater models come with

■ A cable-drive bow-mounted electric trolling motor and its forward/back-toggling foot pedal.

foot pedals due to corrosion problems. Sealed versions of the remote foot pedals, though, are making their way onto the saltwater scene.

Hand Steering. Steering via hand control gives you an immediate response in steering and thrust adjustment. The disadvantage with hand steering is you'll be taking your hand off your rod and reel to make those adjustments. Because hand-controlled models have fewer moving parts for water to get into, they are popular among the saltwater crowd.

Where's the Remote? To be honest, I thought remote-control steering was just another gimmick when it first came onto the market, but a trip with another fishing guide who used it got me thinking differently. Within no time I added one to my existing motor, and I now find it to be irreplaceable for some applications. The small remote—worn on your wrist (which I prefer), belt, or strapped onto a fishing rod—allows you the freedom to control steering, speed, and on-and-off from anywhere in the boat. Remotes can, however, be a little cumbersome for the casting angler since, as with hand control, you have to take your hand off your reel handle to adjust them.

■ Remote-control steering is becoming popular among fresh- and saltwater anglers.

Accessorizing Your Accessories

Automatic steering, which tracks your preset bottom depth or follows a path via a compass reading, is a nice feature for anglers who troll, use a live-bait rig, or cast. You'll spend more time tending rods rather than continuously having to make adjustments with the motor.

A bow-mount motor with a built-in universal sonar transducer is a great feature for those who do a lot of fishing from the bow. These reduce both wire clutter and damage to transducer cables. With the purchase of the correct connector, built-in universal transducers work well with most popular brands of sonar.

Weed-shearing devices, such as Shear Magic, should be considered by anglers who fish often in thick weeds. These attach to the bottom of the trolling motor behind the propeller. As the prop spins, weeds and fishing line are cut up before they wrap up onto and behind the prop.

Pushed from Behind

Transom-mounted electric trolling motors

▥ Close-up of an engine-mounted electric trolling motor.

simply clamp onto the transom. They are popular with small-boat anglers who spend the majority of their time in the stern or who back-troll (a popular ploy among walleye anglers). Transom electric trolling motors are less expensive than bow-mounted motors but offer less power. They work well for basic positioning of a boat and some trolling applications, but offer less control because they push, rather than pull your boat. This is especially noticeable in windy conditions.

It is imperative to match the voltage of transom-mount and bow-mount electric motors if wiring to the same batteries. Trolling motors that draw power from multiple batteries do so equally from all; if one of the batteries is drained lower than the others, the multi-battery unit will have a noticeable loss in power. For example, if a 12-volt transom motor is hooked up to one of the batteries of a 24-volt bow-mounted motor, it will draw power from only the one battery and will reduce the power to the 24-volt system. In other words, the 24-volt bow-mounted motor will have a significant loss of power and battery life.

A high-powered answer to low-powered electric transom motors is motor-mounted electric trolling motors that attach to the lower unit of a main motor. These come in single- and dual-prop models and, like bow-mounts, can be controlled from most anywhere in the boat. Today's dual models offer thrust up to 165 pounds. Like transom electric motors, motor-mounted electric motors should be of the same voltage as bow-mounted if wired to the same batteries.

Power for the Long Run

Having quality marine batteries and correct wiring to those batteries is just as important as the trolling motors themselves.

A cheaply made battery is an inferior battery. Trolling motors should be used only with high-quality, deep-cycle marine batteries made to handle a continuous draw of power rather than a short, high-powered shot of juice, such as a starting battery is made to deliver.

Many boats come with "pro" panels at the bow or in the stern, prewired by the manufacturer between the panel and battery compartment, with a receptacle for the plug of a trolling motor as well as battery/power gauges. With these, connecting your trolling motor to the power sources is a snap.

On smaller craft, however, you may have to add wiring to reach your batteries. First, use nothing less than six-gauge wire when lengthening trolling motor wiring—anything smaller, and the wiring will heat up and short out. Worse yet, connecting to wire of too small a gauge could cause your battery and trolling motor to overheat, causing damage and/or an electrical fire.

Secondly, never wire an electric trolling motor directly to the batteries, but

■ The battery charger on the author's boat (note plug in top right-hand corner) is one of the most convenient accessories an angler can have.

rather have an in-line plug along with the proper in-line fuse. Trolling motors should always be disconnected from power when not in use, especially when charging the batteries. A surge in power during the charging process can blow out your motor's electronics. Also, there is a slight continuous draw of power when a motor's hooked up to the batteries, even when the unit is shut off. If left plugged in, over time, your trolling motor batteries will drain dead.

Charge It!

It is difficult to put into words just how convenient an onboard battery charger is. The process of charging batteries is a complex thing. The perfect amount of amps for the precise amount of time is not only crucial to how many years of service you get from them, but how long it takes them to discharge during use.

Onboard chargers take out all the guesswork and simplify the task. As soon as I am done fishing, for example, I just back my boat in the pole barn, reach in and grab the chargers, and plug in the extension cord—done. Each bank, which charges its own battery, automatically turns off as its charge is complete, eliminating the worry of overcharging (another thing that will shorten the life of marine batteries). When left plugged in, onboard chargers will keep your batteries topped off at full charge during the off-season. If a battery freezes with anything less than a full charge, it will damage it to the point of being rendered useless. Just make sure to purchase an onboard charger that has one bank for each battery you have. Don't skimp.

Here's the Kicker

Kicker motors are 15-horsepower-and-under outboard motors used for trolling and as backup motors for getting back safely to shore. Today's kicker motor, however, is more than just a small outboard motor—some companies are manufacturing kickers with the serious trolling angler in mind. They are geared for power over speed, with built-in self-centering tilt so you don't have to lean over the transom to raise it, and heavy-duty bracketing to take the punishment of running at high speeds over rough water.

Choosing the best kicker for your boat is more difficult than picking out the main motor and electric trolling motor. Unlike other means of propulsion, I believe you can buy a kicker with too much power.

Too large a kicker, for example, will not allow you to achieve an ultra-slow trolling presentation. But at the same time, you don't want to underpower a kicker. There are those moments when you'll need the extra power, such as when trolling into wind or when trying to maintain trolling speed during a turn.

As a rule of thumb, 6-horsepower kickers work well on small, lightweight boats of up to 17 feet. Not only will they idle down to a slow troll, but are light enough in weight so as not to overload the boat. The most popular kicker motor, a 9.9-horse, combines well with heavy boats of 17 to 22 feet. This is the size motor some companies are specifically manufacturing for the trolling angler. This size motor, too, is popular because it can be used as your main power on lakes that have 10-horsepower-or-under regulations—the very reason the 9.9 was designed. Boats 23 feet and larger should be powered by a 15-horsepower kicker.

Kicker Placement

What side of the transom you put your kicker motor on will depend mostly on the size of your boat and the placement of your transducers and speed sensors. On small boats with a single, side console, you'll want it on the passenger side to help even out the weight of the boat when you're fishing alone. It's also a good idea to place your kicker on the opposite side of the transom from where sonar transducers and speed/paddle-wheels are placed, since turbulence from the kicker's propeller will interfere with their signal. On high-transom deep-V trolling boats, such as Great Lakes trolling boats, an auxiliary motor bracket for raising and lowering the kicker motor is suggested. It's much safer to raise and lower a kicker motor when you don't have to lean way over the transom.

The gas supply to your kicker should be a consideration. Most small outboards come with their own portable gas tank; these, however, take up precious room in the boat. With both main and kicker motors now, either four-stroke or oil-injected, it is possible to hook both into one gas tank. Have your dealer or boat rigger hook a separate gas line from each motor into the main gas tank, rather than just putting a tee in the main gas line and running both from one. When a tee connection is used, air will be sucked into the gas line through the unused motor and will make for rough-running motors and possible damage in the long run.

Steering

Once you've decided on kicker size and placement, it's time to consider how you'll be steering it. One of the simplest ways is to steer from the stern, with a hands-on-throttle approach. In this case, I'd recommend a handle extension, as it allows you to steer from both sitting and standing positions. There are several

brands of aftermarket handle extensions available.

For those who'd rather steer via steering wheel, there are several types of detachable steering devices that attach the main motor to the kicker so you can steer in tandem. Some are solid rods that connect the two motors from the front, which are disconnected when the kicker's not in use. Others are self-adjusting steering rods that connect in the rear of the lower units and are able to stay connected even when the kicker's been lifted out of the water.

If you choose to steer your kicker in tandem with your main motor, I suggest installing a separate throttle control so as to make speed adjustments without having to get up and move to the kicker. But have it installed well out of reach from the main motor's throttle control; this is important so there is no mistake of grabbing the kicker's throttle while making a fast run under power of the main motor. I have found it best to mount it directly below the main motor's throttle, near the boat's floor.

As a Backup Plan

Kicker motors come in handy even if you don't do much trolling, as a backup in case the main motor fails, you run low on gas, or your battery drains.

Kicker motors have saved the day for many an angler whose main motors have broken down. It may have been a slow ride back to the dock, but at least it was a ride back.

They've also come in handy due to their fuel economy over high-powered main motors. I know many an angler, low on fuel after a long run out into the Great Lakes, who has come back to port on nothing more than fumes under the power of the gas-efficient kicker.

As for getting get back to port when your battery dies, I've experienced that first-hand. With my kicker wired to the same starting battery as the main motor, all I had to do was pull-start the kicker and let it run for about one minute while its alternator put enough charge into the dead battery to start the main outboard. My kicker saved the day.

Peace of Mind

An outboard motor lock for kicker motors can be a saving grace. Small motors are easy targets of thieves, and there is nothing more violating than when one strikes. A simple $20 lock that covers the kicker's clamp knobs brings inexpensive peace of mind and will save you from frustration later on.

▦ David Scroppo controls his kicker motor via a handle extension while fishing Lake Michigan's West Grand Traverse Bay.

■ When tied off at the bow and positioned near the transom, as fishing pro Mark Brumbaugh has rigged here, a drift sock will take the surge out of a boat trolling with the waves.

Non-powered Devices for Boat Control

There are plenty of accessories for boat control that don't need gas or electricity to make them work. Drift socks (sea anchors), push-poles, and oars are some of the most important.

Sock It to Me

Deploying a drift sock in high wind conditions will slow your boat down to a fishable drift. Drift socks come in many different sizes, all of which serve a purpose.

When I ordered my last two boats, I had an extra cleat attached to each gunwale, centered between the bow and stern, for the sole purpose of tying up a large drift sock. When a large drift sock is deployed from this cleat, my boat achieves a perfect sideways drift. I also have a small drift sock that I tie off to the bow during extremely windy conditions, when gusts grab the bow and push me off course.

Two small drift socks, one tied off each side at the bow with just enough rope that they drift back to the stern—making sure they deploy a few feet ahead of the propeller—will decrease surging of the boat when trolling in large waves.

A large drift sock also doubles as an emergency device. When deployed off the bow—with a length of rope at least 20 feet long so as to allow the bow to ride waves without going under—the drift sock then becomes a sea anchor, and will slow an aimless drift out to sea.

Poles and Oars

A push-pole allows an angler the stealthiest of all approaches when fishing in extremely shallow water. They are the go-to boat-control accessory of saltwater flats anglers, and are even becoming popular with some bass and walleye anglers.

Modern-day push-poles are made of super-lightweight Kevlar material, giving them strength needed to push a heavy fiberglass boat without breaking, all the while being light enough not to sore-arm the person poling.

Oars, too, are lighter and stronger than ever before. Composite materials are the strongest, lightest, and most buoyant.

CHAPTER NINE

Sonar and GPS

Are both sonar and global positioning system (GPS) a necessity on fishing boats? You bet—even for anglers who fish the smallest of lakes and from the smallest of boats.

As I have mentioned with every other accessory—do not try and save a buck when purchasing electronics. Settle for one that "will do," and you won't be happy in the long run. Trust me, it will cost you much more to replace an inferior unit later than it will to buy the one you really want the first time around. How elaborate you want to go with electronics is a matter of personal preference, and most of all, your budget.

Sonar and GPS technology is growing by leaps and bounds. Like home computers, it seems there's always a new-and-improved model on the market. Basically, today's sonar is a computer, with some models having their own hard drives. These are pre-downloaded with information like maps of popular waterways. The added storage also allows you to store more information, such as waypoints and past sonar readings and plotter trails, than ever before. The latest rage is to be able to link, by cable, all your sonar and GPS units together so as to pass information from unit to unit. With additional cartridges, you can also pass this same information from sonar to your home/laptop computer, to study and store information from the day's fishing. You are also able to download upgrades to your sonar from the Internet from manufacturers' Web sites. Unlike home computers, though, the sonar and GPS unit you buy now won't be obsolete in a year and will give you decades of service. Thank goodness!

Both sonar and GPS can be purchased individually or as an all-in-one unit. All-in-ones are nice for small-boat anglers, as they take up less space. I suggest, however, purchasing an all-in-one unit with the largest screen that you can afford. When in split-screen mode—sonar on one side of the screen and GPS on the other—there is a lot of information being displayed, and you'll miss out on detail with a smaller screen.

Many big-water anglers and fishing professionals prefer two separate units—an all-in-one and a separate GPS, for example—just in case. That way if one

■ Fishing pro Mark Brumbaugh watches the screen of his all-in-one sonar/GPS mounted on the dash in easy view from the wheel.

unit fails, they'll at least have one working GPS to allow a safe return home.

As for color display versus monochrome (black and white), I have found color much easier to read. Early color models were hard to read in direct sunlight, but upgrades in screen material and display have made that a thing of the past.

With a color display, it is easy to pick out fish and baitfish from surrounding clutter or bottom. The strength of each signal has been assigned its own color, allowing strong signals to stand out from weaker ones. Contour lines, plotter trails, and icons on GPS are easier to separate from the background with color units.

Sonar—Call It What You Will

You may have noticed I call sonar by its name "sonar" and not a "fishfinder" or "depthfinder." Sure, you can spot fish and tell the depth with these units, but today's electronics show so much more.

Finding structure; deciphering soft from hard bottom; locating the thermocline because you can see dust and plankton in the warm water above the temperature break; these are just a few things you can do with modern sonar. At times, this can be more important information than just spotting fish or knowing where bottom is. Some units even offer anglers the ability to scan, with a photograph-like display, what lurks below as well as out to the sides of the boat.

But all this technology is worthless with underpowered sonar. My rule is to never purchase a sonar unit with anything less than 2,000 watts of peak-to-peak power, as well as the highest pixel count that you can afford, whether you fish deep water or shallow.

A high-powered unit is not only able to detect objects on the bottom in deep water, but also is able to read through tiny particles in the water, such as the above-mentioned plankton, and still be able to see the objects below with full reception. The more power sonar has, the better it can read through even more intense signals, such as weeds, allowing you to see objects and fish within the clutter. A large rock surrounded by soft bottom, or a lone fish, can be spotted in the middle of even the thickest weed bed with a high-powered unit. These units, too, are able to receive information while you're traveling at high speeds, making for a safer ride in unfamiliar water and enabling you to spot structure, baitfish, and fish while the boat's up on plane.

Pixels (picture elements) are the tiny squares that make up the shapes on the screen image. A high pixel count maximizes screen resolution and aids in separating objects such as a fish lying on bottom or within a ball of bait. Again, purchase sonar with as many pixels as you can afford.

Sonar Rigging 101

Two of the most overlooked issues when rigging sonar is making sure that its wiring is separated from all other wiring, and that it is attached directly to a battery with

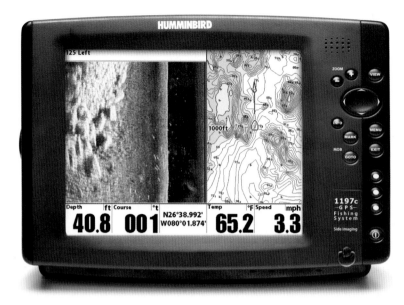

New sonar technology allows anglers to view what lies below and to the side with photograph-like pictures, as shown on the left side of this Humminbird sonar with Side Imaging.
COURTESY HUMMINBIRD

its own connection rather than interfusing with other electronics. The wiring, especially from main and electric trolling motors as well as other electronics, will cause interference. And never wire sonar to trolling motor batteries, as this, too, causes interference every time the trolling motor is engaged. The perfect scenario is to have all electronics wired directly to a separate battery. In the case of small boats where the number of batteries onboard is limited, sonar should be wired to the starting battery. Don't worry about draining the starting battery dead, as today's electronics use very little power.

The next issue is a well-placed transducer. Why? Improper placement of a transducer is the most common cause of interrupted sonar transmission. Basically, sonar works like this: a sound wave, or "ping," is transmitted through the water by the transducer. The wave travels outward,

reflects off objects, bounces back, and is then read by the transducer. The information of the returned signal is transmitted to the sonar and displayed on the screen for your interpretation. If there is any interference in the transmission of the signal, both to and from the transducer, the information to the sonar will be distorted. A transducer will work only when submerged under the water's surface, and turbulence-free water will give it the best reception. Transducers come in two styles: through-hull, mounted in the interior of the boat; and externally mounted puck-style that can be mounted directly onto the transom, on a portable transducer bracket, or onto a bow-mounted trolling motor.

Through-hull transducers, as their name implies, are mounted to the interior of a boat's hull and send and read signals through it. This type of transducer works best with fiberglass boats.

These transducers are held snug to the hull with epoxy. The epoxy, however, must not hold any air bubbles, or the transducer will have poor reception. You'll also want to make sure the transducer is mounted onto solid fiberglass as opposed to an area with foam or wood filler. It is also wise to wrap fiberglass and resin over the entire transducer to make sure it doesn't break free from the hull. Even with a perfectly mounted through-hull transducer, there will be some loss of signal—that is the nature of the beast, due to its indirect contact with the water. Make sure to mount a through-hull transducer in the center of the boat, somewhere between amidships and the stern, so that the area where it is mounted is always in contact with the water, even when the boat's up on plane. Most boat manufacturers suggest locations for mounting this type of transducer. External puck-type transducers must have a smooth flow of water under them to work properly. When mounted at the transom, they should be placed where the water turbulence from hull strakes and

■ This transducer is mounted properly—flush with the bottom of the boat and between strakes.

the propellers of both main and kicker motors won't be an issue.

Depending on its shape, it is important that the bottom of the transducer be mounted flush or slightly lower than the bottom of the boat as well as between strakes, since this is where the water flows most smoothly. Each manufacturer provides detailed instructions for their particular type of transducer. Follow these to a T.

Prop rotation needs to be considered when deciding which side of the transom to mount a transducer. On boats with motors whose prop rotates clockwise, for example, transducers should be mounted on the driver's side so that air bubbles will be pushed down, around, and up the other side, rather than into the face of the transducer.

No Holes about It

The most annoying problem with mounting transducers to a boat's transom is through-hull holes, which, no matter how much you try to make them leak-proof, still leak. One of the best accessories to cure this is a transducer mounting plate—a high-density polyethylene plate large enough for mounting several transducers and speed sensors without ever drilling any holes through the hull. These are nice, too, if you ever want to upgrade your sonar. Old transducers and speed sensors can be taken off and new ones put in their place. They are also convenient if find you need to move your transducer for better reception. Many boat manufacturers are now adding transducer plates of their own in the proper area of the transom, making the chore of proper transducer placement easier than ever before.

Portable transducer brackets are great for small boats or for anglers who move their sonar from boat to boat. These devices are clamped or suction-cupped onto the transom depending on the style. Portable brackets, however, are better left to boats powered by motors 30 horsepower or less, as water turbulence from a high-speed run can pull these free from the boat.

As I mentioned before, many of today's bow-mount electric trolling motors come with a built-in universal transducer, and hooking up sonar to one of these is a cinch with the right connector. Puck-style transducers can be attached to the bottom of trolling motors without built-in transducers with metal hose clamps or plastic zip-ties. Just make sure you allow enough transducer cable to allow the motor to be fully deployed and spin freely.

GPS—Helping You Find Your Way

Had this book been written fifteen years ago, there wouldn't have been much mention of GPS, as these units were found on very few vessels. Today, however, they are standard equipment on fishing boats.

A GPS will aid in getting you to and from the launch safely and in directing you to within feet of previously found structure.

■ The transducer of a bow-mounted sonar on the head of a bow-mounted electric trolling motor. Many of today's trolling motors now come with a universal transducer built in.

Also, by means of a plotter trail, you'll be able to follow the exact trolling path that you caught fish on before. GPS can also decipher boat speed down to one-tenth of a mile per hour—great for trolling.

With the addition of pre-programmed mapping cartridges, you can add information to the background of a GPS screen such as hydrographical (underwater) maps showing breaklines, shorelines, buoy markers, and allowing you to pinpoint your exact position in conjunction to these. These mapping "chips" are one of the most important accessories you can buy for your electronics. The knowledge you gain from seeing the lay of the underwater land and your position relative to key structure is priceless.

GPS works, in general, by gathering information from a network of satellites continuously orbiting the Earth through an internal or external antenna; from this info the GPS determines your location. External antennas must be mounted in an area of the boat where they will not get covered—by a console windshield or open

■ John Semeyn watches the screen of his portable sonar. Note the portable bracket attached to his transom just to the right of his reel.

lid of a storage compartment, for example—and where they will not be stepped on or kicked.

Mounting Your Electronics

First, both sonar and GPS units should be mounted within easy sight of the driver as well as areas of the boat you fish most—at the bow if you fish from there often, or at the stern for those who troll.

The most important accessories for your electronics, by far, are heavy-duty, fully adjustable mounting brackets. The size and weight of electronics are increasing with each new model, and they need mounting systems under them that hold them firmly in place yet can be easily adjusted so as to be seen from most anywhere in the boat.

Electronics take a lot of punishment when you're running in rough water and when towing, so mounting brackets should be bolted through the area they are being mounted—with stainless bolts, washers, and lock nuts—rather than just screwed in.

CHAPTER TEN

Storage for Gear

A place for everything and everything in its place"—an old adage repeated by my grandmother every time her grandkids didn't put something back. This is a motto all boat anglers should heed, as well.

Having fishing, boating, and safety equipment out from underfoot allows you the room to move about, to fish, and fight and net fish while keeping equipment safe from breakage and you and your fishing partners safe from injury.

Boat manufacturers, realizing well-designed storage is a big selling point, are designing more and roomier storage compartments into the interior of their boats. But just because a boat has a storage compartment in every nook and cranny doesn't mean it has the perfect storage configuration. Make sure storage compartments are useful rather than just installed as a sales gimmick, as in "this boat has more storage compartments than our competitor." Mull over the size and placement of every compartment. Can you get a full-sized tackle box in it? Will several adult life jackets fit? What length rods can be packed into the rod locker? Is there room for anchor and anchor line, first-aid kit, fire extinguishers,

multiple marine batteries, tools, and fishing equipment? Does the boat have one live well, or two? Unless you are a serious tournament angler, I'd stick to one live well over two, as the extra one takes up a lot of space that could be storage. A built-in cooler with adequate drainage is a nice feature for food, beverages, and bait. And plan on having an empty storage compartment for your fishing partners' gear, as well.

Consider upgrading to a boat with consoles that have glove boxes, cubby holes for sunglasses and the like, shelving underneath, and/or front or side compartments. You'll fill every storage compartment in your boat—guaranteed.

You should also consider how waterproof, if at all, the compartments are. I suggest at least one totally waterproof storage compartment for cameras, raingear, and other items.

In small boats without storage compartments, something as simple as plastic totes with securely latching lids can be a real space saver. Totes are inexpensive and can be found at most any department store; they are waterproof and hold quite a bit of gear. I'd purchase tall, narrow totes over

■ Fishing pro Kim "Chief" Papineau pulls walleye from his large live well.

short and wide ones, as the former take up less floor space. Dry boxes, too, work well for protecting items like boat registration, flares, and any small safety items. Tall, narrow coolers, rather than long wide ones, are great for small boats. Again, they take up much less floor space.

Open Says Me

The latches of storage compartments are just as important as the compartments themselves. Are handles easy to grasp, twist, lock, et cetera? Can you open the compartment one-handed? Will it be cumbersome to open the storage compartment with gloves on? Will ice and snow render the latches useless? A boat could have the best storage layout ever, but cheap latches and handles will do nothing but aggravate you.

Agonize Over Organizing

Storage goes well beyond what's built into a boat—organizing what goes inside rather than just tossing it in will make you a more efficient angler, too.

▓ Plastic totes with snap-on lids, such as this one at the foot of Michigan's spoon-plug instructor Chase Klinesteker, are inexpensive and great for keeping equipment safe and dry.

Rod storage, or a "rod locker," built into the floor platform or gunwale is one of the most convenient storage compartments there is. Make sure, however, that the locker is well designed, allowing rods to be slid in and out without having to bend them more than just a few degrees. There's nothing more aggravating than having a rod break due to substandard rod storage having been designed into the boat. Most rod lockers have PVC-type tubing to hold individual rods, keeping expensive gear protected and tangle-free. Some designs, however, limit the number of rods you can store in them, while others may have tubing of too small diameter for rods with large guides to fit. Take a rod or two with you when boat shopping, and test out the rod storage.

Small latching plastic organizers are great for keeping tackle, small tools, spare spark plugs, and fuses in order. To make locating items easier, mark what's inside each one in large print with a permanent marker or a label.

Among the most-used storage devices are the cargo nets, which in many boats are located along the gunwales near the bow or along the gunwale at the stern. All sorts of gear can be stuffed in between the netting and the sides where it's easily accessible. Another favored storage device is over-the-seat totes—fabric seat covers with pouches for gear you use often. These really take care of the clutter in a boat, keeping gear easily accessible to all on board.

One of the most annoying items to store is anchor rope, which twists and knots easily, especially if used often. Plastic holders made for wrapping extension cords work well for keeping anchor rope tangle-free. These can be purchased from a hardware store for under $4.

Unruly cable, as on electric trolling motor foot pedals, can be a real headache to store. Double-sided hook-and-loop tape, such as 3M Bundling Wrap, will hold a looped cord tight and keep it out from underfoot. It also works well for bunching wiring or for holding two-piece rods together.

Even storage for something as inconsequential as a drink is important; it makes for a better end to a trip when you don't have to clean up spilled coffee. Whether a built-in or an add-on, boats should have at least four cup holders—one at the bow, two in the middle, and one in the stern.

■ Rod lockers are worth their weight in gold when it comes to protecting valuable equipment. Make sure, however, that the rods are easy in, easy out.

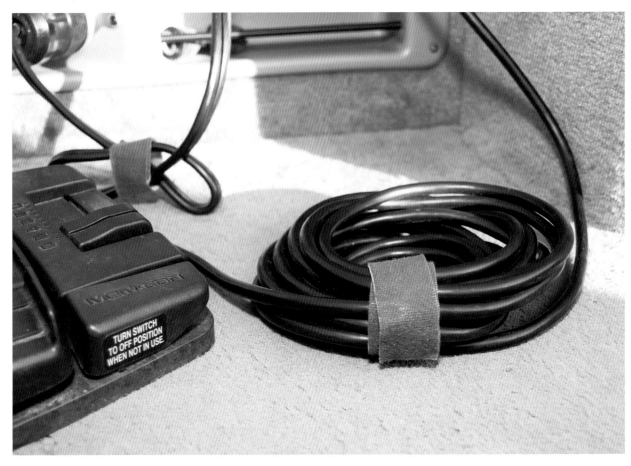

■ Hook-and-loop tape, such as 3M's Bundling Wrap, will tame even the longest wiring.

CHAPTER ELEVEN

Comfort Matters

Are you comfortable right now? Good. And you should be just as contented when fishing. Comfort matters when fishing, whether you are out for only a few hours or an all-day event; you'll be able to endure a long boat ride and concentrate on fishing all day long.

Have a Seat

There is nothing worse than an uncomfortable, flimsy boat seat. In general, the more you spend on a boat, the better seating it will have. On inexpensive models, always check for the option of upgrading seating, and then purchase the best quality you can afford.

It's not just tough material on the outside of the seat that makes for quality seating, but the framing and padding inside. Research; find out what it's made of. High-density foam with an ergonomically correct shape in both the seat and back will make for a comfortable sit, and a heavy-duty frame, preferably made from composite materials rather than wood, will last for years. Make sure, too, that the hinges where the back folds down over the seat are made of heavy-gauge steel—these take a lot of punishment when anglers lean back. On my boat seats—which, because I guide, see more use than the average angler's ever would—the hinges are the first things to go. I have to replace them about every other year.

But even the best-made seat is only going to be comfy if it is at the right height for sitting. Seat pedestals with hydraulic height adjustment rather than a solid tube take care of this problem. Each angler is able to raise and lower the seat to his or her own height, like an office chair. Make sure the pedestals are made of heavy-duty aluminum—there's a lot of torque placed on seat pedestals, especially when riding in high waves. After time, the ends of cheaply made pedestals will collapse and wobble within the floor base.

Spring-Loaded Mounts

The ultimate in seat comfort is to replace the pedestal altogether with hydraulic/ spring-loaded seat mounts, similar to air ride–type seats found in the cab of a semi. Acting as a shock absorber between you and the boat, these devices offer the ultimate sitting comfort in rough water. With these under you, the seat basically stays stationary as the boat rises and falls over the waves. They are good insurance against back injury, so much so that the U.S. Coast Guard is replacing most of their seat pedestals with this type of pedestal. You'll want to make sure these mounts are adjustable to accommodate the weight of each rider. They are pricey but well worth every penny for those who fish on big water. These can be installed later when you save the extra cash.

Take a Load Off

Pro, or "butt" seats—padded, with concave, half-bar-stool shape, attached atop a hydraulic pedestal—are great for the areas of your boat where you will be standing and fishing, most commonly in the bow and stern. These are made for both leaning and sitting. Make sure the hydraulic pedestal is long enough that it can be positioned high on your rear side, up to your waist, yet lowered for a quick sit when your feet get tired.

There are also leaning seats made entirely from composite material—shaped

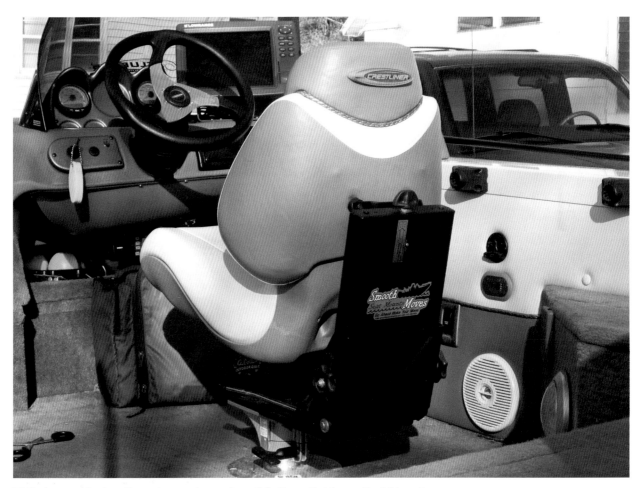

■ Spring and hydraulic seat mounts, such as this Smooth Moves Seat Mount, make for a smoother ride while running in high seas. BRETT KING

like a satellite—which cradle you at the waist. These are very comfortable when used as both a leaning device or laid down flat as a seat.

Underfoot

When fishing, back fatigue can come from more than just poor seating; standing and balancing on hard flooring takes its toll, especially in smaller boats. Rubber floor mats—like those found on cement workshop floors—help remedy this problem.

They'll also help control slips and falls on wet fiberglass floors as well as keep your feet up and out of any standing water.

Overhead Comfort

Bimini covers give anglers protection from the hot glaring sun, a cold wet rain, and everything in between. With biminis, you get what you pay for. Make sure they have a heavy-duty frame as well as fittings and brackets that can take the stress of a strong wind or turbulence during a high-

▓ Scott Pitser rests his feet for a moment while sitting on a butt or pro seat. These seats take up little room in the boat.

speed run. Make sure, too, that they have a heavy-duty sleeve to wrap the bimini in when not in use; otherwise, the bimini can open up like a parachute when on a high-speed run or while towing and can rip free from the boat. On the downside, a bimini top can get in the way when using fishing techniques, especially when casting.

Music Soothes the Savage Beast

Did you know that smallmouth bass like jamming to Jimmy Buffett, walleye will willingly whack a lure to the tunes of '70s funk, and both coho and Chinook salmon slam spoons trolled to the tune of alternative rock? Those are my findings, anyway.

Whether a stereo/CD player belongs in your boat is a personal preference. I've had several clients, after noticing my stereo in the dash of my steering console, shun the idea of any music being played while fishing, no matter the circumstance. They feel anglers should be there to enjoy the solitude of the waterway, not rocking to the oldies. Okay, point taken. But I have a stereo/CD player mounted in every boat

■ Bimini covers get anglers out of the elements, like sun and rain, but limit their fishing techniques. Here, an angler nets a huge muskie caught while trolling—one of the techniques possible with a bimini in place.

I own. There are times when I bore myself and need tunes to bring relief. I like music when fishing with presentations that have downtime, such as trolling.

You'll have to be the judge whether or not music belongs in your boat. If so, buy a marine stereo system—made water resistant and able to take the pounding of rough water and towing.

Oh, What a Relief!

A portable pee cup will bring great relief to an uncomfortable situation and may even save your life. Did you know statistics show that the pant zippers of many recovered male drowning victims were down? They fell overboard when they stood up to relieve themselves over the side of the boat. A portable pee cup makes things that much easier for men and women alike.

And pee cups should go well beyond just an old tin can. There are devices made just for the job that can be purchased for under $5, with a leak-proof lid. These save the day when fishing on lakes with raw waste regulations that require you to dispose of it somewhere other than the lake.

CHAPTER TWELVE

Safety Devices and Equipment

The most important accessories on a fishing boat are the ones that hopefully never get used. Emergency and search-and-rescue devices are not should-haves, but must-haves by law. Tools and extra boat and motor parts are just as important. Whatever you do, don't try to squeak by with the bare minimum of safety equipment that is required by law—splurge. When it comes to your safety, it's better to have and not use than to need and not have.

But before delving into equipment, I want to suggest that you get up-to-date information about the safety equipment required by both federal and state law each and every year. The Internet is one of the best resources we have for immediate information. The U.S. Coast Guard (www.uscgboating.org) and U.S. Coast Guard Auxiliary (www.nws.cgaux.org) are great places to start your search about boating safety. And by all means, take advantage of boating education classes and seminars offered by these entities or reputable organizations in your local area. Have your boat inspected with a Vessel Safety Check—the complimentary check offered

by the U.S. Coast Guard Auxiliary—to confirm it meets both federal and state safety requirements.

It's also a good idea to get up-to-date information from the U.S. Department of Homeland Security (www.dhs.gov), as well. Since 9/11, new regulations have been placed on boating in international waters and in areas around U.S. Army Corps of Engineers dams and waterways. Regulations, too, may change from month to month depending on security threats. Ignorance is not an excuse when it comes to these regulations.

If the Internet's not your thing, then you can get more information by calling these organizations. You can also get information from the harbormasters of major harbors and marinas. Local, state, and federal offices and agencies, such as the County Sheriff, the Department of Natural Resources, and the U.S. Coast Guard, often have booths at consumer boat and sport-fishing shows. Look them up, talk with the staff, and take and read their literature along with informational decals for your boat. I, for one, have several decals on my boat that were given

■ Check with local, state, and federal agencies to be sure you're aware of current safety regulations.

to me by local and government agencies that give detailed information on Mayday procedures, emergency actions, and buoy information. Place these decals where everybody on board can see them, not just the captain, as these quick-reference guides can aid with any problem that arises. Knowledge is your first step in staying safe.

Safety Must-Haves

Accidents, whether caused by another boater or Mother Nature, happen when you least expect them. No fishing boat is totally rigged and ready unless it has the required safety items (and more) allowing you a safe return home. You owe it to yourself as well as others to be prepared for any emergency that may arise.

Vested Interest

At least one life jacket, or personal flotation device (PFD), per person on board is a must. The type of life jacket you should have on board—Type I, II, III, IV, or V, approved by the U.S Coast Guard, wearable and throwable—depends on the water you will be fishing.

- Type I PFDs provide the best buoyancy and may roll an unconscious person face-up. They are required for offshore anglers where rescue may be delayed.
- Type II PFDs will work for near-shore anglers who fish in areas where

rescue will be quick. These can, however, lack the necessary flotation to turn an unconscious person face-up.

- Type III PFDs, such as vests and the newly popular inflatable PFDs, will work in calm waters where rescue will be fast. They will not turn an unconscious person face-up. A side note on inflatables: at the time of this writing, the law requires that these flotation devices be worn at all times.
- Type IV throwable PFDs, such as cushions and ring buoys, are a necessity in every boat. Make sure they are U.S. Coast Guard approved.
- Type V PFDs are special-use devices, such as full-body suits. Some, however, are valid only if worn at all times. Check the label on these.

Make sure you have the proper size PFD for each person on board. Children and small adults can easily slip out of a PFD that is too large. And it is best if you forgo being stylish when purchasing PFDs. For the most part, the bulkier the PFD, the better at saving your life it will be. Gaudy colors, especially high-visibility orange, are easier to see by rescuers. And if not already attached, add some U.S. Coast Guard approved retro-reflective tape to your PFDs, concentrating it on the chest and shoulder areas that will be out of the water and in the view of rescuers. You can find this reflective tape at most boating equipment stores or fire and safety retailers. Print, in large lettering, your boat's registration number on all PFDs with permanent marker. Man-overboard lights that can be pinned onto a PFD and automatically turn on when flipped upright are always a bonus.

Snuff Said

Fire extinguishers are required onboard by law. These devices can be confusing to purchase because there are so many types. Be sure to purchase one that is not only a type B, but is labeled "Marine Type USCG." Size I and II extinguishers will fit within the storage compartments of most fishing boats. Externally mount or store the extinguisher (whatever is required by law for your size boat) within a compartment in an area easily accessible yet away from where fires could potentially start. You can't get to a fire extinguisher in an area that is already on fire. An area away from gas motors and batteries is suggested.

Another in-case-of-fire add-on to consider is a brass on/off fuel valve. These should be attached in-line on the fuel line and away from the motor. This allows you to turn off the gas flow to the motor in the case of fire. You can purchase these at boating and auto parts retailers.

And while it's not directly related to fire safety, a carbon monoxide detector is a good idea for large boats with enclosed cabins, for example, some large Great Lakes trolling boats. As always, better safe than sorry.

Being Seen and Heard

Visual distress signals (VDS) include items such as flares (at least three), an electric distress light, and orange distress flag. Flares have an expiration date and must be within this date to be valid. Check the batteries in any electronic distress device at least twice a year, and carry extra batteries for them.

Sound-producing devices like an athletic whistle and air horn are required, too. An air horn is suggested even for boats equipped with a built-in push-button–type horn. Marine batteries will short out in a boat that is taking on water, rendering an electric horn worthless.

As for storing emergency supplies, all should be packed in a waterproof box marked "Emergency Equipment" in large lettering and should be within easy reach somewhere in the middle of the boat, such as under a steering console.

Beyond What's Required

Safety equipment goes well beyond what's required by law, and should include quick fixes for breakdown and injury.

A tool kit containing pliers, screwdrivers, and wrenches like a spark plug wrench and a prop-nut wrench or socket that fits the nut, can save the day when your boat or motor breaks down. You should also carry extra race, pins, emergency prop, and spark plugs.

Go through your boat, determine the type and size of all fuses of electronics and motors, and carry spares of each. A blown fuse is the most common cause of electrical failures and should be the first thing you check when any problem occurs.

Other items, such as an extra drain plug, plastic zip-ties, electrical tape, vinyl repair tape, and extra stainless nuts, washers, bolts, and screws for those "just-in-case" moments, all packed into a divided tackle box, are suggested as well.

Have a first-aid kit on board. No, not just a couple adhesive bandages and a travel pack of aspirin, but a real first-aid kit containing ice packs, bandages of every size and shape, rubber gloves, tapes, and ointments. You can purchase a compact, well-stocked first-aid kit from warehouse retail stores for around $20.

A powerful flashlight or rechargeable spotlight will aid you in getting back to the dock at night. You may want to add a cigarette lighter–type power source, for accessories with a DC power cord, somewhere on the dash if your boat doesn't already have one. Most rechargeable spotlights come with this type of charger, and the receptacle may come in handy when you need to recharge in a pinch. Just remember to keep your boat's motor running—allowing the motor's alternator to keep charging the battery—while using powerful spotlights, as they draw a lot of juice.

Hello?

There's always controversy over whether a cell phone even belongs in a fishing boat; many anglers feel you are there to fish and get away from such devices. But cell phones are the perfect apparatus for requesting help in an emergency situation. If you don't want to hear it ring, then turn the ringer off. But keep the phone on while you're on the water, so time isn't wasted while it boots up and searches for a close-by cell tower. And pack it in a waterproof, talk-through bag to protect it from rain or an accidental drop in the drink. These dry bags are available at most boat supply retailers for under $15.

Breaker, Breaker

Every boat should have a marine radio with proper antenna, or at least a handheld version, on board. Marine frequencies are constantly being monitored by agencies such as the U.S. Coast Guard. Like cell phones, marine radios should be turned on at all times. By sending a distress call via marine radio, you stand the chance of earlier rescue by nearby boaters, as well. I have personally been the first responder to a boat taking on water because I heard their distress call through my marine radio. My being there before emergency help arrived kept a bad situation from becoming worse. Hopefully the same will happen to me if the table ever turns.

Utilize Magnetic North

As I mentioned back in chapter 9, GPS is a great tool for getting you back to the dock. Don't, however, overlook the old-fashioned compass! A magnetic compass can get you back to shore when electronics fail. And just as with every other piece

■ All boats, even if rigged with the latest in GPS technology, should have a magnetic compass on board and in plain view of the driver.

of safety equipment, do not buy a cheap model, as a low price usually indicates an inferior product. I had one compass, for example, that would continuously spin from the vibration of the boat every time the motor was put in gear. To get a reading, I had to stop the boat. You can get a well-made compass for $40 to $50.

Pump It Up a Notch

All boats should have at least one bilge pump installed. The installation of a second pump is something all boaters should consider. In most situations, boats take on water faster than a single bilge pump can keep up with. At least one of the bilge pumps should be automatic, triggered to turn on when water lifts its floating toggle switch. A bilge suddenly turning on is the first indication there is a problem. Failure of through-hull fittings, such as a livewell hose, for example, are just one of many causes of boats taking on water. An automatic bilge pump will start pumping water as soon as a leak forms; otherwise, a leak may go unnoticed until it's too late. This allows plenty of time to turn on the other bilge pump and either fix the problem or make a run back to shore.

Small boats without a battery-powered bilge pump should have a manual bilge pump. It's also a good idea to have a manual bailing device, something with a handle, on board as well. This goes for boats with bilge pumps, too. Nothing fancy; a milk jug with a handle and a wide-cut opening will do.

Up, Up, and Away

Ever wonder how you'd get back into the boat if you were to fall out while fishing by yourself? A boat ladder, connected and ready to go, is the answer. Many boat manufacturers are now adding folding ladders to the transoms of their boats as standard equipment. On boats without these, the addition of a rope ladder is suggested. Make sure, however, that these are already connected before you get onto the water. A rope ladder in your boat's storage compartment will do you no good when you are floating around in the lake.

Tow, Tow, Tow Your Boat

Water-skiing is probably the farthest thing from an angler's mind—but a water-skiing Y tow harness should be in every angler's boat. These harnesses work well for towing other boats without causing damage to your own. There's a lot of torque put on a single cleat when towing a heavy boat with a rope, and they can be ripped right off the gunwales. When using a water-ski harness, attached onto the eyelets of a transom, the torque is distributed equally throughout the transom and both sides of the boat. As for a rope for towing a broken-down vessel, you can either carry a water-skier tow rope or use your anchor line.

Anchor—A Weighty Choice

An anchor and anchor line should be thought of more as safety equipment than just a means of staying put over a likely fishing spot.

As discussed in the first five chapters, anchors come in many different shapes and styles. Some are specialized for specific types of use—such as those found on drift- or saltwater flats boats. All boats, however, should be equipped with a heavy fluke-style anchor, as these give a solid hold in emergency situations.

These anchors should be attached to a 3-foot section of steel chain (to add weight) to keep the top of the anchor down. The anchor needs to be attached to the chain with an anchor shackle, snap-shackle, or quick link—not a snap hook or a carbine hook, as anchors can easily slip free from these. Attach the chain to a minimum of 100 feet of anchor line at least ³⁄₈ inch in diameter. Make this connection by splicing a metal thimble into one end of the line (or purchasing a line with the thimble already spliced), forming a loop in which to shackle the free end of the anchor chain.

Why so much anchor line? To anchor properly, you should have at least (and this is the very least) triple the amount of anchor line out for the depth of water you are anchoring in. This allows enough angle in the line for the anchor's flukes to grab hold, and to allow the boat's bow to ride up over large waves without pulling the anchor free or pulling the boat under. Refer to chapter ten, on how to properly store anchor line.

▥ A boat ladder is your only way back into the boat if you fall out while fishing alone.

CHAPTER THIRTEEN

Fishing Accessories

The word I want you to think of while rigging your boat with the following fishing accessories is "efficient." Ask yourself: How efficient will the accessory be if I mount it here?

Figuring out the best spot to rig fishing accessories within your boat will be the hardest thing you do. Unlike the aforementioned accessories that must be mounted in specific spots for them to work to their maximum efficiency, the following have no real right or wrong place to mount them—it's more a matter of personal preference than anything else. There are, however, two rules to remember before you pull the trigger and send that drill bit spinning.

Rule one: Take your time, lots of time, when deciding where to mount each and every piece of equipment. This may seem backward, but it is best to get out in your boat and go fishing before you attempt to permanently rig the tools of the fishing trade. I know you are in a hurry to get everything rigged, but don't push it. Trust me on this one. The decisions you make on where to rig fishing accessories will affect how your boat fishes the rest of its life.

Once you have an idea where you want an accessory, you'll need to get in the boat and put that accessory in every conceivable spot in that particular area. Slide it over an inch here and an inch there; think about the pros and cons of that accessory in that place. Will it be in the way when you cast? Will storage compartment doors be affected? Will it affect other accessories you want to put in the same area? Will your mooring cover fit properly when this accessory is in place?

It is best if you rig your own fishing accessories; this is your boat and you'll be the one fishing from it, not the professional boat rigger. But at the same time, don't hesitate to have friends come over while you're rigging and get their opinions. They may notice a problem you overlooked or may suggest other alternatives that didn't come to mind. And by all means, if you hire someone else to rig your boat, make sure you are there while they are doing it. Again, it's your boat and you want everything where you want it, not where the boat rigger thinks is best.

Rule two: Reinforce everything. Unlike major accessories, some smaller items may not have heavy-duty hardware, and their instructions may not emphasize enough the importance of proper mounting. If the item calls for size X screws, then beef them up to size Y, or replace the screw altogether and mount the accessory through fiberglass, aluminum, or wood with nuts, washers, and bolts, if possible; it'll be that much more secure. And add support to the backside of whatever it is you are attaching it to; thin marine plywood or composite material works well for this. Rough water and towing take their toll on mounted accessories, and over time they will eventually come loose. There's nothing worse than being on a fishing excursion and having an accessory mount break free, especially if it was a case of "If I'd only done it right the first time, it would never have failed."

Rod Holders

Rod holders are the quintessential tool of fishing boats, so never be a penny-pincher when it comes to purchasing them, or lackadaisical when mounting them.

Purchase rod holders that are fully adjustable, removable, and that are easy in, easy out for all styles of rods and reels. Buy extra bases and mount them in several areas of the boat so that you can move the holders from spot to spot depending on fishing technique. It is best to match brand and style of all rod holders rather than having a hodgepodge. This allows you to move them throughout the boat,

base to base, as needed. It is also easier to make adjustments when they all work the same.

Positioning and Mounting

Figuring out where to place rod holders will be the most agonizing thing you'll do. You'll need to get in the boat, sit down in the seats, and ponder: Are your rod holders going to be within easy reach from a sitting and/or standing position? Make sure they are. When rods are in them, are the reel handles and rod butts going to be in the way of other seating, storage lids, downriggers, outboards, and the like? Make sure they are not.

Remember Rule 2, reinforce everything? There's an awful lot of torque placed on rod holders when they are in use. Add support behind the gunwale or transom area and screw or bolt the holders into it. Several anglers I know have lost gear—rod, reel, line, lure, and all—to large fish due to improperly mounted rod holders.

If your boat has rails, then rail-mount rod holders are suggested; you don't have to bore new holes into the boat, and depending on the technique you are using, they can be moved into different positions along the rail.

One of the handiest items to come to market of late is track systems. These tracks—mounted onto gunwales and transoms—make equipment, such as rod holders, sonar, GPS, and even downriggers, all more adjustable and removable than ever before.

Getting Down with Downriggers

Downriggers are standard tools for accurate depth control while trolling. Whether you choose a manual hand-crank or electric model to lift and lower the heavy lead ball (known as a cannonball) is a personal preference that depends how often you'll be using them and how much money you are able to spend.

Electric downriggers are pricey, but are well worth it if deep-water trolling is your main thing. With a push of a toggle switch, they automatically raise and lower the 10-pound-or-heavier cannonball. This allows an angler to multitask—to reel in fish while the ball is being automatically brought back to the boat, for example. Hand-crank downriggers offer weekend warriors, who may troll only a few times per year, an inexpensive means of enjoying the sport.

Rigging 'Riggers

There is nothing more cumbersome to work with than a downrigger mounted in the wrong place. And when it comes

■ Rod holders are the quintessential tool of fishing boats; think long and hard on their placement in your boat.

▓ Mounting track, such as this from Bert's Custom Tackle, on the gunwale of this boat allows anglers to attach, adjust, and detach all kinds of fishing equipment with ease.

to torque placed on a gunwale or transom, downriggers win out over all other accessories.

Rigging 'riggers starts with proper placement. You'll be working over these devices—literally leaning on and over them—so it is imperative to position them where there is plenty of room to stand. This can be a difficult process in smaller boats, as not only platforms, chairs, and storage compartments need to be considered, but having access to underneath

where the downrigger is to be mounted is crucial. You'll need plenty of room to reach your arm up and under during the process of adding reinforcement to the mounting area.

Instead of mounting directly to gunwales and transoms, mounting platforms that run from gunwale to gunwale across the stern are preferred by many anglers. Both downriggers and rod holders can be mounted onto these, and the unit can be easily put on for trolling applications and

■ Downriggers should be rigged where they aren't in the way of storage compartments or over platforms, and where they are comfortable to get to. Here, John Manville trolls with downriggers on Lake Michigan's West Grand Traverse Bay.

■ Fishing pro Greg Yarbrough (left) attaches an in-line planer board to his main line while fishing Lake Michigan's Green Bay.

taken off for other styles of fishing. These platforms, however, may hamper the use of some storage compartments or can get in the way of accessing outboard motors.

The height at which you mount your downriggers needs to be considered. They should be mounted about waist to belly high—no more, no less. Pedestal mounts between the downrigger and its base are suggested on boats with low gunwales and transoms. Downriggers mounted to gunwales need swiveling bases under them so

you can swing the 'rigger in parallel to the boat for launching, loading, and towing.

Mounting downriggers will test both your rigging skills as well as your patience—plan on it being an all-day event.

Planer Boards and Mast

More and more, we anglers have realized that fish don't live just down deep—they suspend high in the water column, too. Planer boards, as their name implies,

■ A long-handled net with large-diameter hoop is just as important as any fishing accessory bolted to your boat. Here, guide Hugh Witham prepares to scoop up a steelhead from Michigan's Big Manistee River.

plane outward from the boat and get your lines and lures out of the path of your boat and into the face of unspooked fish. There are two types of planer boards to choose from—in-line and full-sized boards.

In-line planer boards are small devices—a little larger than your hand—that clip directly to your line and pull it outward from the boat. A sturdy rod holder is about the only other accessory needed with these.

Popular among big-water anglers, on the other hand, are full-sized planer boards. These are best deployed via a planer board mast mounted to the bow. With a planer board mast and its hand-crank reels spooled with 150-pound-test braided line, you can let out and retrieve full-sized planer boards with ease.

Planer boards not only ride out, but also back from the boat, so masts need to be rigidly attached to either the bow platform (where a bow-mounted trolling motor would go) or onto the floor as far forward toward the bow as possible. Most use a permanently mounted base secured tight to the floor or platform. Some anglers have tried to forgo mounting the base plate, and instead have masts custom welded onto seat pedestals, which are snapped into place in the seat base. Eventually, this system fails as the torque placed on a planer board mast eventually works the connection loose.

Don't Overlook These!

Fishing accessories go well beyond large-ticket items. There are several accessories every boat should have that don't need to be screwed or bolted in place.

Go Nuts over Nets

Ever notice the fishing nets for sale at garage sales? There's a reason the owners are trying to get rid of them—they were too small to get the job done right.

Every boat should have a large-hooped, long-handled net on board—regardless of the size of fish being targeted. A net with a large-circumference hoop and long handle allows you to scoop the wildest thrashing fish without having to lean far over the side.

In some cases, you may want more than one net onboard. Many Great Lakes anglers, for example, carry two large nets, since often more than one fish is hooked

at a time. Rather than try and dump out a thrashing salmon, with hooks flying about and tangling into the net, they use the second net to land the other fish.

In the Introduction, I mentioned landing my biggest fish to date—a 50-inch muskie—with nothing more than a tiny, short-handled trout net. I should never have landed that fish. That I didn't flip that 12-foot rowboat while attempting to land that fish is a miracle of its own. Since that day, I've carried the largest net my boat can handle.

Make sure, though, that nets are out of the way, yet within easy reach. On boats where casting is not an issue, nets can be stored upright in rod holders or in a ring device that stands them up on end. A small 3-inch section of PVC pipe screwed onto a gunwale near the bow will work fine for this. Otherwise, tuck the net somewhere out of the way, with the hoop up under a console or held vertically between a small cooler and gunwale, for example.

Visual Aid

No boat is complete without a set of marker buoys. Despite what's being said about the pinpoint accuracy of GPS, I'm here to tell you it is easier to stay on structure marked with a marker buoy than while watching the screen of a GPS unit. One of the biggest mistakes anglers make is to tuck their buoys deep inside a storage compartment. Instead, these should be in a holder and out where you can grab them easily while fishing. When you mark structure, you just grab one and toss it overboard. When done, you can scoop it back up with that long-handled net.

Another accessory well worth a look is a device for holding fishermen's tools such as hook sharpeners, pliers, wire cutters, and the like. My favorite, by far, is a magnetic holder made by Rapala. This type of device should be mounted out in the open, within easy reach of all anglers onboard.

Aluminum or composite rulers for measuring the length of fish should be mounted in areas easily accessible, near live wells if catch-and-keep is your thing or along gunwales if you'll be releasing most of your fish. Having these measuring devices out in the open allows you to quickly measure and put the fish wherever with little harm to the fish.

Underwater cameras/viewing systems are making their way to the forefront with anglers. These are great tools for learning

just what lurks below, deciphering right before your eyes just what it is your sonar is marking. Underwater cameras are great for entertaining kids aboard your boat and educational as well. There are models that permanently attach to your boat—with a large screen mounted onto the dash, and a foot control to raise and lower the camera unit over the side—as well as portable units small enough to easily stow away in storage compartments. As technology changes, the price of these underwater viewing devices is coming down, making them affordable for all anglers.

Peruse the marine-supply catalogs or retailers, and you see there are plenty of fishing accessories in today's market for you to fill your boat with; however, I would forgo overdoing it. As I mentioned earlier in this book, it's not the angler with the most equipment, but the angler who has just the right amount of equipment and in the right place to make them a more efficient angler, who wins.

CHAPTER FOURTEEN

Trailers and Towing

Rarely do I guarantee anything, but I will step out on a limb and say that over time, without a doubt, towing your boat with a substandard trailer will do more damage to your boat and its accessories than anything else during its lifetime—guaranteed.

How can that be? A poorly made trailer rides rough. Its thin steel frame bends under the weight of a heavy boat and motor, and the torque placed on the hull from all this twisting will loosen rivets in aluminum, crack fiberglass, and wear holes through wood. And a low-grade suspension can't compensate for the pounding from the pavement. Continuous jarring will hammer components, such as windshields and seat pedestals, to a frazzle and shake boat accessories loose. Because today's towing vehicles ride smoother than ever, you don't realize the beating the boat and motor are taking back there. Loading and unloading your boat at the launch will be a bear with an inadequate boat trailer, as well.

A quality, heavy-duty boat trailer, on the other hand, cradles your boat securely while it's being towed. Its heavy-gauge steel won't twist when rolling over back-road hills and dales, and neither will your boat. Heavy-duty suspension and quality full-sized tires absorb the shock of ruts and potholes and reduce the jolt to your boat and accessories, making for a smooth ride all around. And getting the boat on and off at the launch will be a snap.

What to Look For

As I mentioned earlier about outboard motors in chapter 7, you'll also need to beware of the boat trailers that accompany the too-good-to-be-true boat, motor, and trailer packages. These combos are often packaged with inferior trailers to keep monthly payments low. Always upgrade the trailer and its accessories to the highest quality you can afford. You won't be sorry.

Trailer Style

There are two different styles of trailer when it comes to how the boat sits on the trailer and how it's loaded and launched—roller and bunk.

Roller Trailers. A roller trailer is the easiest to get a boat on and off, as the boat's

■ Rollers are the easiest to launch and load a boat with; however, long-distance travel can damage a boat's hull over time due to little surface area touching the boat.

hull rolls on top of wide spinning polymer wheels. Boats move so easily on rollers that you must never disconnect the bow/winch strap until the boat is over water. I have seen plenty of boats shoot off a roller trailer at the launch and crash onto the dry cement ramp. Ouch! The damage caused can be unfixable.

A roller trailer is not a good choice for heavy vessels or for long-distance travel. Little surface of the hull is in contact with the rollers, and damage will occur at these contact points over time. Aluminum hulls will stretch and dent, and fiberglass hulls will crack. But roller trailers are well suited for lightweight boats, especially for those launched often at unimproved boat ramps or in the bush of the backwoods. They are also suitable for boats that are moored or docked more than towed.

Bunk Trailers. Bunk trailers, on the other hand, offer the most support to a boat's hull. The entire hull is supported by the full length of the bunk. These trailers come with either a single or double pair. Heavy boats should always be supported by two pairs, as the weight is evenly distributed by all four bunks.

Launching and loading from a bunk trailer can be difficult in shallow water. A short-term answer to launching in low water is to spray silicone over the entire surface of all bunks. This helps even the heaviest boat slide on and off easily.

A lasting solution is to accessorize bunks with composite pads that are infused with non-stick products like Teflon, which will ease launching and loading, as if there were rollers underneath. Again, never unclip the bow/winch strap until over water when using these pads; otherwise the boat could slide off unexpectedly.

Rollin', Rollin', Rollin' . . .

The next thing to consider is whether you need single or dual axles under the trailer. In general, boats 19 feet and larger must have dual axles under them due to the weight of the vessel. Dual-axle trailers provide a smoother ride, and having multiple tires on each side offers peace of mind in case one fails. One disadvantage, however, is that dual-axle trailers are difficult, if not impossible, to turn and move by hand once unhooked from the tow vehicle. This is something to consider if you'll be moving your boat around in a garage.

Trailer tires should be upgraded to the best money can buy, no matter what style trailer you choose. Tires are the only thing holding your trailer to the road, and low-grade models aren't stable and can easily blow. Radial tires offer a smoother ride and wear more slowly than bias-ply tires. A trailer that bounces and wobbles from side to side while running bias tires will lose these characteristics when you replace them with radial tires. Tips: A trailer that pulls poorly could also be caused by having improper tongue weight. The weight at the tongue should be 5 to 7 percent of the entire load. Weigh the rig at a truck/weight area and make adjustments from there. Also, check trailer tires for uneven wear and damage every 1,000 miles, at least, and more often if stored in direct sunlight.

Both tires and rims should be the largest diameter the trailer can handle. Small-diameter tires make thousands more revolutions than larger ones, which not only quickly wears down tread, but heats and wears out bearings as well.

As for bearings, they come either packed with grease or in a reservoir filled with oil. Which one you choose is a matter of personal preference. Both require yearly maintenance and several inspections per year. Grease-packed bearings should be refilled at least once a month.

Add-ons, such as Bearing Buddies—caps with Zerk-type fittings for adding grease—replace standard dust caps. These keep dirt and water from entering into the bearings and also make refilling the hub with grease easy. Don't, however, think that these devices make it so that you do not have to regularly inspect and re-pack your bearings! Water is the enemy of both grease and oil, and will eventually enter into your hub, mix with bearing grease, and break it down.

Tip: You can thwart some of the water entering your bearings by taking time to allow the hubs to cool off at the boat launch before dunking that trailer into the lake. A sudden drop in pressure occurs within the hot bearing housing when it hits cold water, thus water gets sucked in.

Accessorizing for Safety and Longevity

Accidents not only happen while boating, but while towing to and from the water,

as well—even a quick maneuver to avoid an accident while pulling a heavy trailer, for example, can cause a mishap. Not only do some of the following accessories help keep the unforeseen from occurring, but also keep the boat tight to the trailer while towing and will decrease the wear and tear damage to both your boat and trailer for years to come.

Spare Me

If a new trailer does not come with a spare tire and carrier, then by all means, that's the first thing you need accessorize it with. Just make sure the spare matches size and diameter, and if possible, the same brand and model as the main tires. And if

▓ Dust covers with Zerk fittings, such as this Trailer Buddy with Trailer Buddy Bra, allow you to easily fill bearings with grease as well as protect them from dirt and water.

■ A spare tire and carrier should be your first trailer accessory. This one's been attached to the tongue and acts as a step in and out of the bow of the boat.

the spare tire carrier is not permanently attached, consider moving it to an area on the trailer where it can serve multiple purposes. For example, I have attached mine to my trailer's tongue, opposite the winch handle, just under the boat's bow, so I can use it as a step for getting in and out of the boat when I am attaching the winch strap.

Tie-downs

There's more to properly towing a boat than just winching it onto the trailer and taking off down the road. Both boat and motor should be strapped down to the trailer, and accessories clamped down to reduce vibration, thus damage.

Boats need to be strapped down to the trailer to avoid shifting when riding around corners, over bumps, and in case of an emergency ditching. And a boat strapped down tight won't bounce on the trailer as the trailer and boat will hop together over bumps, allowing the trailer's springs to take the shock.

The winch strap will keep the bow tight, while transom tie-downs keep the stern snug. Some deluxe-model trailers have ratchet tie-downs permanently attached. These can be purchased aftermarket, as well.

Don't, however, get a false sense of security that bow and transom straps will keep the boat on the trailer during a major accident. In severe accidents, the metal S-hook of a strap will straighten out and the boat will part ways with the trailer.

This happens in roll-over accidents as well as rear-end and head-on collisions.

A safety strap—a chain, wire, or webbed strap between the winch and bow—should be connected whenever towing to keep the boat from lifting off the trailer in case the winch strap fails. There's a lot of lift to the bow when it's being towed at high speeds, and it could rise, then flip off the trailer.

There should also be two lengths of chain at the tongue, as well. These chains, crossed to form an X, will hold the trailer tight to the tow vehicle in case the coupler should accidentally detach from the ball. The reason for the X shape is to allow the detached trailer tongue to rest on the crossed chain, rather than having the tongue dig into the ground, catching, and flipping the whole rig on top of the tow vehicle.

Avoiding Bounce

All motors at the transom, as well as bow-mounted electric trolling motors, should be stabilized to keep them from bouncing. Over time, damage to the both boat and motors will occur if they are not.

Transom Savers hold a motor's lower unit tight to the rear of the trailer. As their name implies, these devices will save the transom from damage due to the motor continuously bouncing up and down while being towed.

The head of an electric trolling motor, on the other hand, should be held tight to the gunwale with a stabilizer bracket.

■ Tie-down straps at the transom will keep the boat snug to the trailer, allowing the trailer to take the shock of the road, not the boat.

There are several models on the market, all which seem to work well.

Give Me a Brake

Did you know it takes at least three times the normal distance to stop when towing the average boat, motor, and trailer, and even more with heavier boats? Trailer brakes make coming to a halt that much quicker, and save wear and tear on your tow vehicle's brakes. Federal regulations state that any trailer and load 3,000 pounds and over must be equipped with brakes at the axle. But brakes are a good idea on trailers hauling less weight than that. Many trailer manufacturers are making brakes standard equipment on their trailers.

Not too long ago, surge brakes were the only type of brake found on boat trailers, as electricity and water just don't mix. But electric brake technology has changed, and there are power brakes on more boat trailers than ever before.

Electric brakes, wired in conjunction with the tow vehicle's wiring, engage

■ All trailers should have a safety chain at the bow. This can be added later if the trailer is not equipped with one.

only when the tow vehicle's brake pedal is depressed. Most new tow vehicles are coming prewired for electric trailer brakes from the manufacturer, so that the trailer only needs to be plugged in for travel. Older vehicles can be easily wired at most car repair shops.

Surge brakes, on the other hand, work when the tow vehicle's brakes are applied and the forward momentum swings a pendulum, which engages the trailer brakes. Something to think about with surge brakes, however, is that they can be a problem if you have to back a trailer uphill or creep slowly down, such as on a steep driveway, in that gravity will swing the pendulum forward or back and engage the brake.

Easy Loading and Unloading

The most frustrating occasion for any avid angler is the time spent at the boat launch—waiting to launch or load, and then being scrutinized by others as they wait for you. There are several trailer accessories you can add on to your trailer to speed your time at the launch.

Side bunks, or guide-ons, help guide your boat onto the trailer and then keep

■ A set of safety chains at the tongue, seen here attached properly–crossed with an X–are a must on trailers.

it centered as you pull it out—great when you are loading by yourself.

An electric winch will pull a boat up onto a trailer quickly and is especially nice at launches where power-loading—thrusting the motor forward to drive the boat onto the trailer—is not allowed.

Step plates, which attach to the tongue and on the side of the trailer, are nice when you have to walk out onto the trailer to hook up the boat to the winch strap, rather than having to balance only on the narrow frame. Some trailers come with these as standard equipment.

On trailers that tow boats up to 18 feet, the wheeled jack at the trailer tongue should, at the least, be able to lift 1,000 pounds. On boats any larger, I suggest tongue jacks with double wheels that can lift 1,500 pounds. It's not that you'll be lifting this much weight at the tongue, but that heavy-duty jacks can withstand the torque of rolling an unhooked trailer, and their wheels will spin easier and the

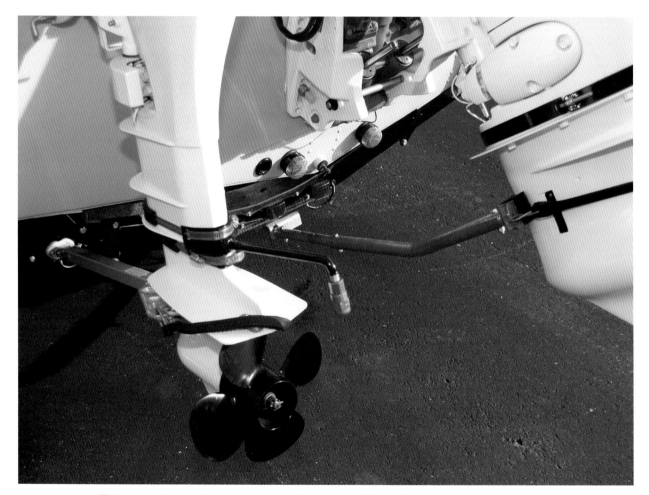

■ Transom Savers keep motors from bouncing while towing, reducing wear and tear on the boat's transom.

tongue can be swung around without much effort.

Protect Your Investment

Boats and motors are expensive, no doubt. You should rig your trailer with accessories to protect them from wear and theft.

Boat covers are well worth the expense, as they not only keep the elements from damaging the interior of your boat, but traveling versions of mooring covers can increase your gas mileage when towing.

Boat covers should have lots of straps or snaps along their side to keep them tight to the boat. If loose fitting, a mooring cover will flap in the air turbulence and shred, especially around accessories such as trolling motors and rod holders. Mooring covers that come with boats will more than likely need to be customized to fit over or around added fishing accessories; most covers are a standard size and shape, designed for boats without such accessories. A tight-fitting mooring cover reduces wind resistance and drag, and that can increase your gas mileage by nearly 2 miles per gallon—quite a savings over a long-distance haul.

Trailer accessories are expensive, and thieves know it. Can you imagine coming back to the boat launch and finding your tires, if not your whole trailer, gone? It happens more often than you may realize. Locks for tires, including spares, will discourage would-be thieves. Coupler locks for the trailer hitch should be on every trailer, as well. Lug-nut and coupler locks are well worth the money.

Be Prepared

Trailer failure never occurs in a convenient area or at the opportune time. What I call a "trailer kit"—a plastic tote pre-packed with tools and extra parts that's always in the back of the tow vehicle—can save the day when things go awry.

When you purchase a new trailer, find out the exact model number of the bearings and buy an extra set. Some bearings are special-order, and it may take days to find and then have them shipped. You don't want your rig sitting roadside that long, if at all. Blown bearings can ruin bearing races and hubs, as well, so you should have extras of these packed in the trailer kit, too. Bearing grease, tools for changing out bearings, and a full roll of paper towels should also be in the tote.

Although modern-day trailer lights don't burn out like their predecessors, you should always have a spare. Most boat trailer lights now come as one waterproof unit, so replacing a burned-out light takes more effort than just screwing in a light bulb; wire clippers, crimps, and a crimping tool will be needed. A handful of extra fuses and bulbs for running lights are suggested, as well.

A set of folding wheel chocks will come in handy for those times you unhook. A short floor jack—one small enough to fit not only under a low-slung trailer but a low-slung trailer with a flat tire (lower to

■ Built-on step plates make walking out onto the trailer easier and safer. Trailers without them can be accessorized with after-market plates.

the ground than with a full tire)—should be in the trailer kit, too.

Tips for Backing That Trailer

I thought I would end this book with some tips for backing up a boat trailer—the most frustrating process for both the angler doing the backing and those waiting for them at the launch.

It is best to use your tow vehicle's mirrors rather than turning around in the driver's seat to look out the back window. Mirrors do not lie: When they show there's room to spare, there's room to spare; if it looks like you are about to hit something, stop.

Learning to back up while using mirrors can be hard at first; you have to learn to turn the steering wheel the opposite direction you want the trailer to go. An old farmer's trick I learned years ago for backing up with mirrors is to place your hands on the bottom of your tow vehicle's steering wheel and when you want the trailer to go left, move your hands left; when you want it to go right—well, you get the picture.

▧ Trailers that haul boats up to 18 feet should have at least a 1,000-pound jack, 1,500 pounds for larger craft.

Practice, practice, practice! A buddy of mine once said, "The World's Fair and boat launches are where all the stupid people go." Don't be one of those stupid people. Take the time to perform backing-up procedures in an abandoned parking lot or in your home's driveway before going to the launch. Over time, backing will became old hat, and you'll enjoy that fishing trip, and all those accessories you rigged onto that fishing boat, more than ever.

■ Mooring covers protect a boat from the elements and can increase gas mileage when towing vehicles.

APPENDIX

Some Major National Marine Suppliers

West Marine
www.westmarine.com

Boater's World
www.boatersworld.com
www.boatersworldstores.com

Hamilton Marine
www.hamiltonmarine.com

Cabela's
www.cabelas.com—click on Boating

Bass Pro Shop
www.basspro.com

River Marine Supply
www.rivermarinesupply.com

Or enter Marine Suppliers into your preferred Search Engine.

About the Author

David A. Rose was born in Michigan's southern Lower Peninsula in 1967. In 1976 his family moved to the Traverse City, Michigan, area—the perfect place for someone with a passion for hunting, fishing, camping, and all aspects of life in the outdoors. He has resided there ever since.

In 1986 Dave not only graduated from Traverse City Senior High School, but also earned the rank of Eagle Scout with the Boy Scouts of America and was inducted as a Vigil Honor Member of the organization's Order of the Arrow. He attended Northwestern Michigan College. He married the love of his life, Carol, in 1991, and she's been putting up with him ever since.

Dave's passion for teaching others how to enjoy the outdoors launched his

career as a writer, photographer, seminar speaker, and fishing guide in 1997. For more information check out his Web sites at www .wildfishing.com and www.davidarose.com.